Upon seeing all the devastation brought by Typh
old daughter asked a theological question which
"Why did God allow the storm to happen?" Thi
our hearts, "Why, O God?" This commentary on
affirmed the validity of our very human grief in the midst of losses, but at the
same time, it pointed out biblical resources to draw upon to strengthen us
in our journey of faith. I find it a very rich reflection to help us deepen our
Christian faith in our own Asian context.

Charlie E. Labarda, MD
Survivor of Typhoon Yolanda,
Church Council Chairperson (2013–2015), UCCP Tacloban City,
Founding Chair, BUHAT Tacloban, Philippines

When terrible natural disasters such as the Asian Tsunami and the fierce winds
and storm surge of Typhoon Yolanda (Haiyan internationally) happen, the
inevitable question arises: "Where was God?" "How could a just God allow
this?" Federico G. Villanueva takes us through an engaged reading of the
poetry of the book of Lamentations against the specific context of Typhoon
Yolanda's devastation and anguished "Why" question. Villanueva's sensitive
interpretation succeeds in demonstrating that to read Lamentations "in a
detached, objective, uninvolved manner is to be like the 'friends' and 'lovers'
of Lady Zion who showed her no comfort when she most needed it."

Helen R. Graham, MM, PhD
Institute of Formation and Religious Studies,
and Loyola School of Theology, Ateneo de Manila, Philippines

This simply written study on lament (the central theme of Lamentations),
though scholarly, is deeply devotional and warmly applied to the inexplicably
tragic destruction of lives and property particularly wrought by the world's
worst typhoon, Haiyan (Yolanda), that swept the central section of the
Philippines. As brought out in the book, God's dealings can be puzzlingly
mysterious – but "his compassions never fail."

Rodrigo Tano, PhD
First Area Dean, AGST–Philippines
Senior Professor, Alliance Graduate School, Philippines

Asia Bible Commentary Series

LAMENTATIONS

Asia Bible Commentary Series

LAMENTATIONS

Federico G. Villanueva

General Editor
Federico G. Villanueva

Old Testament Consulting Editors
Yohanna Katanacho, Tim Meadowcroft, Joseph Shao

New Testament Consulting Editors
Steve Chang, Andrew Spurgeon, Brian Wintle

© 2016 by Federico G. Villanueva

Published 2016 by Langham Global Library
an imprint of Langham Creative Projects

Langham Partnership
PO Box 296, Carlisle, Cumbria CA3 9WZ, UK
www.langham.org

Published in partnership with Asia Theological Association

ATA
QCC PO Box 1454 – 1154, Manila, Philippines
www.atasia.com

ISBNs:
978-1-78368-191-4 Print
978-1-78368-193-8 Mobi
978-1-78368-192-1 ePub
978-1-78368-194-5 PDF

British Library Cataloguing in Publication Data
A catalogue record for this book is available from the British Library

ISBN: 978-1-78368-191-4

Cover & Book Design: projectluz.com

To the victims and survivors of Typhoon Yolanda/Haiyan

CONTENTS

Topics

SERIES PREFACE

In recent years, we have witnessed one of the greatest shifts in the history of world Christianity. It used to be that the majority of Christians lived in the West. But now the face of world Christianity has changed beyond recognition. Christians are now evenly distributed around the globe. This has implications for the interpretation of the Bible. In our case, we are faced with the task of interpreting the Bible from within our respective contexts. This is in line with the growing realization that every theology is contextual. Our understanding of the Bible is influenced by our historical and social locations. Thus, even the questions that we bring into our reading of the Bible will be shaped by our present realities. There is a need therefore to interpret the Bible for our own contexts.

The Asia Bible Commentary (ABC) series addresses this need. In line with the mission of the Asia Theological Association Publications, we have gathered Asian evangelical Bible scholars in Asia to write commentaries on each book of the Bible. The mission is to "produce resources for pastors, Christian leaders, cross-cultural workers, and students in Asia that are biblical, pastoral, contextual, missional, and prophetic." Although the Bible can be studied for different reasons, we believe that it is given primarily for the edification of the Body of Christ (2 Tim 3:16–17). The ABC series is designed to help pastors in their sermon preparation, cell group leaders or lay leaders in their Bible study groups, Christian students in their study of the Bible, and Christians in general in their efforts to apply the Bible in their respective contexts.

Each commentary begins with an introduction that provides general information about the book's author and original context, summarizes the main message or theme of the book, and outlines its potential relevance to a particular Asian context. The introduction is followed by an exposition that combines exegesis and application. Here, we seek to speak to and empower Christians in Asia by using our own stories, parables, poems, and other cultural resources as we expound the Bible.

The Bible is actually Asian in that it comes from ancient West Asia and there are many similarities between the world of the Bible and traditional Asian cultures. But there are also many differences that we need to explore in some depth. That is why the commentaries also include articles or topics in which we bring specific issues in Asian church, social, and religious contexts into dialogue with relevant issues in the Bible. We do not seek to resolve every tension but rather to allow the text to illumine the context and vice versa, acknowledging that in the end we do not have all the answers to every mystery.

May the Holy Spirit who inspired the writers of the Bible bring light to the hearts and minds of all who use these materials, to the glory of God and to the building up of the churches!

Federico G. Villanueva

General Editor

AUTHOR'S PREFACE

Bible commentators do not usually share their own experiences in their interpretation of the text. However, I am firmly convinced that until we see our own experiences in the light of the biblical text and vice versa, we have not yet understood the text. This applies to any book of the Bible, but it has a particular relevance to the book of Lamentations. This book cannot be understood apart from the experience of suffering and the agony that goes with tragic experiences. So in this commentary I have tried to relate my people's experience of the devastation of the city and region of Tacloban by Typhoon Yolanda to the experience of the Jewish people who mourned the destruction of Judah and the city of Jerusalem by the Babylonians. Together we will read Lamentations in "collective solidarity with a suffering people."[1]

There is historical precedent for this. The Jewish people themselves do not restrict the relevance of this book to their ancestors' experiences when Jerusalem was destroyed. They recognize that it speaks to all their other experiences of destruction. As Asian believers who accept that the Old Testament is part of the Word of God that comes from Yahweh, the Father of our Lord Jesus Christ, we too believe that the book speaks to us in our suffering in a region of the world that has to deal with the twin realities of poverty and spirituality.

Speaking from my own cultural context in the Philippines, suffering is one of the things that draws our people closer to God. In times of disaster, there is no one else to whom we can turn. The God addressed and prayed to in the book of Lamentations is very real to us. We do not read the book as outside observers; we share the same spiritual sentiment as the poet of Lamentations. That is why I do not refer to the God spoken about or spoken to in Lamentations as "the deity," as some commentators do. The God to whom the laments are offered in the book is the same God to whom I cry out. This commentary is informed by the perspective of a believing community who consider their relationship with God as the very foundation of their existence.

---

1. This "collective solidarity" is "the way back to Lamentations." Zachary Braiterman, "Lamentations in Modern Jewish Thought," in *Great Is Thy Faithfulness?: Reading Lamentations as Sacred Scripture*, ed. Robin A. Parry and Heath Thomas (Eugene, Or: Pickwick Publications, 2011), 95.

ACKNOWLEDGMENTS

This commentary could not have been written without the prayers and support of family, friends, and institutions. Langham Partnership International, which supported my PhD studies, kindly extended its support through the writer's grant program. Chris Wright, the International Director of Langham, has been a great encouragement to me. The Langham Literature team have worked closely with ATA Publications to make sure this commentary becomes a reality. I would like to make special mention of Pieter Kwant, Luke Lewis, and Isobel Stevenson, who carefully read and edited the final manuscript against tight deadlines.

Dr. Rodrigo Tano, a leading Filipino evangelical theologian, helped me see the importance of reading from within our own context. I received great help in doing this from Bro. Karl Gaspar, CSsR, who has kindly given me permission to use material from his book, *Desperately Seeking God's Saving Action: Yolanda Survivors' Hope Beyond Heartbreaking Lamentations*. His work as an anthropologist among survivors of the typhoon has helped me as a biblical scholar to understand the book of Lamentations from our own context of suffering. Sr. Helen Graham, MM, one of the editors of Gaspar's book, graciously read my manuscript and made insightful comments. The Institute of Studies in Asian Church and Culture (ISACC) has made it possible for me to visit Tacloban and see for myself what happened in the aftermath of Typhoon Yolanda. I thank Dr. Melba P. Maggay, president of ISAAC, for inviting me to be part of the team, which did a psycho-spiritual workshop for the survivors. It was there where I understood the words of Jesus on the cross, "My God, my God, why have you forsaken me?"

I have benefited from the comments and suggestions of Tim Meadowcroft and Yohanna Katanacho, Consulting Editors of the Asia Bible Commentary Series. As Publications Secretary for the ATA, I am grateful for the support and encouragement of the ATA General Secretary, Dr. Joseph Shao, and of the whole team: Dr. Theresa Lua, Alex Lactaw, Marlene Riate, and Bubbles Lactaoen.

They say that writing is one percent inspiration and ninety-nine percent perspiration. This is literally true in the Philippines, given the hot and humid weather. So I thank the Society of the Divine Word Seminary in Tagaytay through its rector, Fr. Mike Layugan, SVD, and dean, Fr. Randy Flores, SVD, for welcoming me. The combination of the nice weather in Tagaytay and the warm community in SVD created an environment conducive for writing. I also wish to thank Asbury Theological Seminary for their writer's grant that enabled me to spend a month on the campus in 2013. Trinity College, Bristol, also provided a space for me in 2014 so I could do some research. Closer to home, the Asia Pacific Nazarene Theological Seminary in Antipolo and the Loyola School of Theology in Ateneo de Manila have provided a room for me as well as access to their library for my research. I would like to thank Dr. Huang and the Faith, Hope, Love Prayer Institute and Seminary for giving me the privilege of teaching Lamentations in one of their classes. I have greatly benefited from interactions with my students.

But there is more to life than just writing. So I would like to thank those who gave me space to breathe and remain human. My Wednesday group fellowship played an important role in doing this. So I thank Ruben and Glo, our hosts, for their hospitality, and the whole group – Ana, Marlene, Zeny and Arnold, our facilitator – for wonderful times of sharing, prayer, and fun. My DVD group with Benjie and Abbie De Jesus and Alwin and Johanna De Leon has also provided friendship and spiritual support through my writing journey.

For Filipinos, the family is always a part of everything we do. I am thankful to my parents, Bishop Butch Villanueva and Melita Villanueva, for their love, prayers, and support. It was from them that I first learned how to pray. During my writing, Arsenia Casingal, my mother-in-law, has stayed with us. I have received great insights through my conversations with her and by simply being with her. Her daughter, Rosemarie, my wife, has been my companion not just during the writing of this commentary but through my own times of lament. *Salamat mahal.*

Federico G. Villanueva,

Cainta, Rizal

May 2016

LIST OF ABBREVIATIONS

BOOKS OF THE BIBLE

Old Testament

Gen, Exod, Lev, Num, Deut, Josh, Judg, Ruth, 1–2 Sam, 1–2 Kgs, 1–2 Chr, Ezra, Neh, Esth, Job, Ps/Pss, Prov, Eccl, Song, Isa, Jer, Lam, Ezek, Dan, Hos, Joel, Amos, Obad, Jonah, Mic, Nah, Hab, Zeph, Hag, Zech, Mal

New Testament

Matt, Mark, Luke, John, Acts, Rom, 1–2 Cor, Gal, Eph, Phil, Col, 1–2 Thess, 1–2 Tim, Titus, Phlm, Heb, Jas, 1–2 Pet, 1–2–3 John, Jude, Rev

BIBLE TEXTS AND VERSIONS

Divisions of the canon

NT	New Testament
OT	Old Testament

Ancient texts and versions

LXX	Septuagint
MT	Masoretic Text

Modern versions

ESV	English Standard Version
NIV	New International Version
RSV	Revised Standard Version

Journals, reference works, and series

AB	Anchor Bible
ABC	Asia Bible Commentary
ABD	Anchor Bible Dictionary
ANET	Ancient Near Eastern Texts
BibInt	*Biblical Interpretation*
Int	*Interpretation*
JBL	*Journal of Biblical Literature*
JSOT	*Journal for the Study of the Old Testament*

OTE	*Old Testament Essays*
SBL	Society of Biblical Literature
VTSup	Vetus Testamentum Supplements
ZAW	*Zeitschrift für die alttestamentliche Wissenschaft*

INTRODUCTION

"Outside, the sword bereaves, inside, there is only death."
(Lam 1:20)

When the winds got stronger, my mother suggested that we leave our house and find a more secure place to stay at the height of the typhoon. But we all convinced her that it was safer to stay inside our house as we saw the movement of the wind outside. It got stronger and the trees were being blown away. We all stayed in the big room of our house. My mother told us to pray and we all joined her praying that we would be safe. But looking outside, we saw the situation worsening. Then the roof of our house was blown away and we all became very afraid. We rushed inside the bathroom. My mother told us to remain in the bathroom whatever happens next. There we continued praying, asking God to protect us. Then the flood waters came and we all got separated.[1]

The story told above comes from one of the survivors of Typhoon Yolanda (International name: Typhoon Haiyan) – the strongest typhoon in recorded history. In 2013 it devastated the Samar-Leyte region and surrounding towns, leaving thousands dead. Ground zero was the city of Tacloban. "It was as if God had abandoned the place," a young photographer told me. He went there a week after Yolanda struck. "The place was like a war zone," he continued.

He was not the only one to link storms and wars. So did people in ancient times. We see this in the ancient literary genre known as "city laments." These are compositions bewailing the destruction of a city. For example, the "Lamentation over the Destruction of Ur,"[2] which laments the fall of the city

---

1. Karl M. Gaspar, *Desperately Seeking God's Saving Action: Yolanda Survivors' Hope Beyond Heartbreaking Lamentations* (Quezon City, Philippines: Institute of Spirituality in Asia, 2014), 112.
2. The following is taken from Samuel Noah Kramer, "Lamentation over the Destruction of Ur," in *ANET*, ed. James B. Pritchard (Princeton, NJ: Princeton University Press, 1969), 455–463.

of Ur to the Elamites, speaks of "the evil storm" of destruction in words that often mirror the events in Tacloban:[3]

- "the storm that annihilates the land"
- "the boats of the city it attacks (and) devours" (In Tacloban, the storm surge swept a ship into houses.)
- "The evil wind, like the rushing torrent, cannot be restrained" (A woman from Tacloban told me of the terrifying roar of the wind and of the battering rain which stung like thorns.)
- "In all its streets, where they were wont to promenade, dead bodies were lying about"
- "My ox in its stable has not been . . . ed,[4] gone is its herdsman" (Before the storm, the *sari-sari* stores were full of groceries, but all was carried away by the waters.)
- "My daughters and sons verily . . . have been carried off" (An elderly woman described how her husband was swept away by the waters together with his pedicab.)

The people of Tacloban could join with the ancient writer who lamented:[5]

The storm which knows not the mother, the storm which knows not the father,
The storm which knows not the wife, the storm which knows not the child,
The storm which knows not the sister, the storm which knows not the brother,
The storm which knows not the weak, the storm which knows not the strong,
The storm on whose account the wife is forsaken, on whose account the child is forsaken.

Not only do the city laments use storm imagery to depict the violent destruction of cities by their enemies, they also associate God with what has happened. Writing about the use of such imagery in another ancient lament known as "The Lament for Sumer and Ur," Dobbs-Allsopp comments:

---

3. It should be noted, though, that while the ancient writers used the imagery of storms as metaphor for their experience, it was not a metaphor for the Yolanda victims; they tell exactly how horrible it was. Sr. Helen Graham, MM, has rightly observed this in a personal correspondence.
4. The "ed" represents a verb in the original language but is uncertain.
5. Kramer, "Lamentation."

"Whatever one may deduce about the historicity of these enemies in the laments, their invasion is indisputably a literary motif, analogous to that of the evil storm, symbolizing the destruction of Sumer. As such, storm and invasion imagery become mixed, and the storm sometimes seems to serve as the chief metaphor for the foreign invasion initiated by Enlil [a Mesopotamian god]."[6]

Though the writer of Lamentations does not use storm imagery, elsewhere in the Hebrew Bible such imagery is used to describe manifestations of Yahweh (see, for example, Jer 47:2 and Jer 51:42).[7] So we would not be wrong to compare the way in which the Babylonian army invaded Jerusalem in 586/587 BC to the violent waters roused by the storm surge of Typhoon Yolanda. "The Philippines is both geophysically and meteorologically one of the world's natural hazard 'hot spots.' According to the Belgium-based Centre for Research on the Epidemiology of Disasters (CRED), which has compiled one of the most comprehensive records on the occurrence of natural hazards in the world since 1900, the Philippines experiences more such events than any other country."[8] In this commentary, I read the book of Lamentations from our own experience of disasters. In so doing, I am following in the footsteps of Archie Lee, who drew on the tragedy that took place in Tiananmen Square in 1989 in his short commentary on the book of Lamentations.[9]

READING LAMENTATIONS FROM THE CONTEXT OF DISASTER

In the past, scholars read and commented on the biblical text as if they did not come from any particular place or context. But we have increasingly realized that contextless interpretation is impossible. Every theology and every interpretation of the Bible is rooted in a particular context. Interpreters of the Bible describe this insight in terms of a shift in emphasis from the "world behind the text" and the "world within the text" to the "world in front of the text."

---

6. F. W. Dobbs-Allsopp, *Weep, O Daughter of Zion: A Study of the City-Lament Genre in the Hebrew Bible* (Roma: Editrice Pontificio Istituto Biblico, 1993), 56–57.
7. Compare Ibid., 62.
8. Greg Bankoff, *Cultures of Disaster: Society and Natural Hazard in the Philippines* (London: RoutledgeCurson, 2003), 31.
9. Archie Chi Chung Lee, "Lamentations," in *Global Bible Commentary*, eds. Daniel Patte and Teresa Okure (Nashville, TN: Abingdon, 2004), 226–233, see esp. 226–228. He describes the Tiannamen tragedy as one of the "national calamities" of Asia.

When we are dealing with a book like Lamentations, we cannot be unengaged. How can we not feel the suffering described there? We must become like its poet-author who sees the tears in Lady Zion's eyes and her outstretched arms as she pleads for mercy. To read Lamentations in a detached, objective, uninvolved manner is to be like the "friends" and "lovers" of Lady Zion who offer her no comfort when she most needs it (see Lam 1:2). We cannot read Lamentations in the abstract. It must be read from within real historical situations: "No matter what theoretical approaches one uses to analyze the text, it had to be created and/or performed by 'real people' in specific historical context, regardless of how uncertain we are with those details."[10]

In filling in the details of my own "specific historical context" I draw on the reflections and research of Karl Gaspar, who spent four months in Tacloban immediately after Typhoon Yolanda.[11] He and a team of workers from the Catholic church came to accompany the people in their grief and facilitate psycho-spiritual healing, or as he puts it, "We were in the disaster-affected areas to be present to the survivors and primarily do whatever we can to accompany them in their grieving and healing process."[12] His work is a good example of doing theology from the ground. He is a trained anthropologist, and draws on what he knows of the social sciences, but he supplements them with theology. He was the first to attempt to use the book of Lamentations as a resource in helping survivors of disaster.[13]

Our recent experience with Typhoon Yolanda, in particular, is relevant because it shows strong similarities with what we find in the book of Lamentations. Like Jerusalem, Tacloban and the surrounding area were devastated.

> An estimated 12.2 million people (2.6 million families) were reported to have been affected by the disaster . . . About 4.4 million people (930,000 families) were displaced, with 400,000 people housed in more than 1,500 evacuation centers . . . there

---

10. Nancy C. Lee, "The Singers of Lamentations: (A)Scribing (De)Claiming Poets and Prophets," in *Lamentations in Ancient and Contemporary Cultural Contexts*, eds. Nancy C. Lee and Carleen Mandolfo (Atlanta, GA: Society of Biblical Literature, 2008), 35.
11. Gaspar, *Desperately Seeking*.
12. Ibid., xviii.
13. I am speaking from my own context in the Philippines, though I am not aware of any work in Asia doing the same thing. It should be noted, however, that Gaspar did not focus directly on the book of Lamentations but on the book by Kathleen M. O'Connor, *Jeremiah: Pain and Promise* (Minneapolis: Fortress, 2011).

were 5,982 reported fatalities . . . A further 27,022 people were reported injured, with 1,779 persons still missing.[14]

"My God, my God why have you forsaken us?"

The responses to the devastation were also similar. The following comment by the former mayor of Davao City now turned president of the country, Rodrigo Duterte, when he visited Tacloban captures what some of us felt: "I think God was somewhere else when the typhoon hit. God must [have been] somewhere else or he forgot that there's a planet called Earth."[15] My own Facebook post at the same time expressed much the same feeling as I watched the news reports coming in: "*Diyos ko, Diyos ko, bakit mo kami pinabayaan*" [My God, my God, why have you forsaken us?].[16] The same feeling of divine abandonment pervades the book of Lamentations. What pains Lady Zion more than anything else is that her Lord, whom she considers her true comforter, has left her (see Lam 1:16). At the very end of the book, the people are still crying, "Why do you always forget us? Why do you forsake us so long?" (5:20). Those who faced Yolanda had the same response:

> As Yolanda struck with its furious winds and horrific floods, they desperately sought their God who would save them. In the aftermath of the catastrophe when they realized the depth of their despair, they cried out to God in their lamentations.[17]

"Restore us to yourself"

But in spite of their lamentations, the people of Jerusalem never gave up on God. Lamentations is a highly religious book. Its main concern is the restoration of the people's relationship with God. "Zion will be consoled if and only if her chosen partner-in-dialogue, the one she simply and nakedly calls *my Lord* and *Yhwh*, sees her as she sees herself."[18] (161). As the poet cries,

---

14. NEDA report; quoted in Gaspar, *Desperately Seeking*, 10. Many believe the number of casualties could be even higher.

15. Bella Cariaso, Banders Inquirer. Online: www.bandra.iinquirer.net/39867/wala-any-diyos-nang-nanalasa-si-yolanda (quoted in Gaspar, *Desperately* Seeking), 101.

16. My home is far from the region devastated by Typhoon Yolanda, so I was not affected directly. But my experience of Typhoon Ondoy, which inundated our village, allowed me to identify with the experience of those in Tacloban.

17. Gaspar, *Desperately Seeking*, xix.

18. John F. Hobbins, "Zion's Plea That God See Her as She Sees Herself: Unanswered Prayer in Lamentations 1–2," in *Daughter Zion Her Portrait, Her Response*, eds. Mark J. Boda, Carol J. Dempsey, and LeAnn Snow Flesher (Atlanta, GA: Society of Biblical Literature, 2012), 161.

"My eyes will flow unceasingly . . . until the LORD looks down from heaven and sees" (Lam 3:49–50). Even when they felt the punishment was excessive, they still clung to God. Despite the pain of seeing little children dying, the poet still exhorts Lady Zion to "pour out your heart like water in the presence of the LORD" (2:19). And at the very end, their prayer remains, "Restore us to yourself, LORD . . ." (5:21).

We see something of this same attitude in the people of Tacloban. I will never forget the photograph of a drenched woman standing in front of what used to be the church, now swept away by the flood. The image epitomizes the strong role of "faith in our culture. In Pablo/Bohol/Tacloban, people run to the churches."[19] At the height of the typhoon, as the winds raged and the storm surge wreaked havoc, everyone was crying out to God. Prayer filled the city both during and after the typhoon. Gaspar states: "In the course of our conversations with them, there was only one refrain as they spoke about the early morning incident of 8 November – they prayed to the Almighty with all their heart as they battled debris to remain afloat, and once they found themselves alive when the waters subsided, they expressed deep gratitude to God for having survived."[20]

"*Jesus, tama na po*" [Jesus, please enough]

Such prayers are important because they reveal our view of God. Theologizing is not only the work of professional theologians. Even ordinary people theologize, especially children. We can see this in the prayer uttered by a little girl as the waters rushed into the evacuation center where her family had sought refuge:[21]

> "*Jesus, tama na po*" [Jesus, please enough]

I think we can draw out the following beliefs/theology about the disaster from her prayer:

- First, God is viewed as the one causing the disaster. That is why the girl asked God to stop it ("*tama na po*" = enough).
- Second, the girl sees God as the savior, which is why she is calling for his help.

---

19. Here Gaspar cites a paper by Vidal.
20. Gaspar, *Desperately Seeking*, 60.
21. A staff member of ISACC who talked with this girl shared this story to me. The girl uttered this prayer as her mother shouted to her to go to the second floor to escape the inrushing water. As she prayed, she felt something or someone lifting her and so lived to tell her story.

- Third, the girl was praying to God not only because she views him as the Savior but also because she feels that it is already too much – "*tama na po*" [please enough].
- Fourth, God is addressed as "Jesus."

A similar theology pervades the book of Lamentations. God is viewed as the cause of the destruction of Jerusalem. The people believe it was God who commanded the Babylonians to destroy the city (1:17). It was he who rejected all the warriors of Judah (1:16), causing them to experience disgrace before their enemies (1:6). Yet in spite of the fact that God is seen as the one who caused the destruction, the people still call to him for help. "Look and see," cries Lady Zion (1:9, 11). Even at the very end of the book, the people hold on to God as the one whom they believe still cares for them (see Lamentations 5). They may describe God as being "like an enemy" (2:4–5), but he also remains like a father to whom they turn when they are fatherless and widowed (5:3). The following words about the survivors in Tacloban can also be applied to the people in Jerusalem: "The survivors would blame God for this catastrophe, but they would also find the need to keep God alive."[22]

Though there is no confession of sin in the little girl's prayer cited above, this element is also present in the prayers of our people. Gaspar cites the prayer of Siony de Vera: "*Lord tama na po, tama na po. Patawarin mo po kami kung ano man ang aming nagawang mga kasalanan*" [Lord, please enough, please enough. Forgive us whatever sins we may have committed].[23] The same prayer for forgiveness (*patawarin mo kami*) has been posted on the ship that was swept ashore by the storm surge, crushing houses and killing many. Similarly, the people in Lamentations confess that it is because of their sins that destruction has come upon them: "The LORD has brought her grief because of her many sins" (Lam 1:5). Lady Zion herself admits, "The LORD is righteous" (1:18). This is an acknowledgment that God is justified in his actions and they are in the wrong. This attitude is characteristic of the prayers of confession found elsewhere in the Old Testament (see Ezra 9, Neh 9, Dan 9). The central element of the prayers of confession is the admission of guilt (see comments in Lam 1:5, 8–9, 18 below).

---

22. Gaspar, *Desperately Seeking*, 104.
23. Ibid., 109. The English translation is my own.

"Why do you forsake us so long?"

But the admission of guilt does not prevent people from expressing what they feel, though culturally, we are not direct in our expression of pain. Going back to the prayer of the little girl, her sense that the suffering is excessive is expressed as well: "*tama na po*" [please enough]. Similarly, in Lamentations, despite the admission of sinfulness, the people feel that the punishment is too much, however indirectly this is communicated. For instance, Lady Zion's speech to passersby reveals the sense that it has gone too far.[24] She asks, "Is any suffering like my suffering?" (1:12). Later, Lady Zion becomes more direct: "Look, LORD, and consider: Whom have you ever treated like this?" (2:20). At the end of the book the people asks God, "Why do you always forget us? Why do you forsake us so long?" (5:20).

The question "why?" is the characteristic cry of lament, as is clear even in the book of Lamentations. It should be noted, however, that the expression of lament is not always direct. Just as many traditional Asians communicate indirectly, so the lament in the book of Lamentations is expressed indirectly. In fact, there is no direct use of the word "why?" until the third chapter when the prayer turns into a communal lament. It seems that the poet is unable to lament directly to God on his own; he needs the community. The only extended, direct lament is the communal lament at the end of the book (Lam 5). For the rest, the poet hides behind the figure of Lady Zion, using her to communicate his emotions. Even his complaint about the suffering of little children is expressed by the personified Lady Zion (Lam 2:20) and not by the poet directly. The expression of lament in this book is thus similar to the way we communicate. As Asians, we do not express our complaints directly. We are not assertive by nature, although this is changing as a result of social media. Still, we do not express our feelings of hurt directly. We do it through indirect means.[25]

We can note Gaspar's experiences of this: "Fr. Gerry Matriano, CSsR, a member of the mission's coordinating team, shared that he was very much surprised that in the countless conversations he had with the survivors, no one expressed any anger towards God or thought of Yolanda as God's

---

24. The sense of "grievance" is an important thread in Lamentations. See Leslie C. Allen, *A Liturgy of Grief: A Pastoral Commentary on Lamentations* (Grand Rapids, MI: Baker, 2011), 20–21.

25. Melba Padilla Maggay, *Pahiwatig: Kagawiang Pangkomunikasyon ng Filipino* (Quezon City: Ateneo de Manila University Press, 2002).

punishment."[26] Yet though the people did not lament, Gaspar himself did. In his journal, he wrote: "Where is your love and compassion when you seem to be absent in this landscape; do you turn into a parent who abandons your children and disappear from their midst?"[27] When he heard the news of another approaching typhoon soon after Yolanda, Gaspar prayed: "Why so soon? We can't help but ask this question, dear God. Why so soon that another typhoon – named Basyang – has found its way through the Central Visayas route?"[28] Nevertheless, praying like this remains uncommon. When I asked the team from the Asian Theological Seminary who visited Tacloban if they had heard laments, they said no one lamented. This leads us to the question – Why do we not lament?

WHY WE DO NOT KNOW HOW TO LAMENT

The following reflections on why Filipinos in general do not lament in the way that the people do in the book of Lamentations are based solely on my own observations, not on detailed anthropological research. That is something I hope to undertake in the future. Nevertheless, I believe that these reasons do influence many, though not all, of my fellow Filipinos, as well as believers in other parts of Asia.

Faith in the suffering Jesus

The little girl's prayer above ("Jesus, *tama na po*") was addressed to "Jesus." She comes from a country where the most popular image of Jesus is the crucified or suffering Christ.[29] So in her prayer, in which she calls God "Jesus," the girl is simply voicing what many of our people have come to believe about God, namely that he is one with us in our sufferings through Jesus. This view enables us to cling to the God who is also our Savior and Father even in times of disaster.

A deep sense of guilt or sinfulness

I once asked a group of twenty-five teachers to write their own prayers after a lesson on prayer. Almost all of them wrote prayers of confession or petitions for forgiveness. Our feeling of guilt and sinfulness are deeply engrained.

---

26. Gaspar, *Desperately Seeking*, 109.
27. Ibid., 221.
28. Ibid., 223.
29. Benigno P. Beltran, *The Christology of the Inarticulate: An Inquiry into the Filipino Understanding of Jesus the Christ* (Manila: Divine Word Publications, 1987), 117.

Those feelings are reflected in the other prayer mentioned above, *"patawarin mo po kami"* [forgive us our sins]. We agree with Green, who comments that "since all are sinners, what is extraordinary is not that some suffer in a world ruled by God, but that anyone is spared the divine wrath."[30] But does the fact that we are indeed sinners mean that we can never lament?

Strong belief in fate

Capaque writes: "Filipinos can endure suffering because *walang nangyayari na hindi kalooban ng Diyos* [nothing happens apart from the will of God]."[31] This includes disasters. We see this in the words of a woman who lost her daughter in Typhoon Yolanda:

> The water rose very quickly. The members of my family did our best to survive; my husband and son were able to climb up to the roof. I struggled to swim and was able to hold on to a post and realized later that my daughter, Joyjoy also tried to swim. I tried my best to save myself . . . I prayed to God – Lord, whatever it is that you want with our lives now, thy will be done. *Diyos ko, ikaw na po ang bahala sa amin* [My God, I entrust to you our lives].[32]

Part of our worldview is that everything that happens has been ordained (*itinakda*) by God.

Our experience of colonization

Our historical experience of colonization may also have contributed to our inability to lament. More than four hundred years of colonial rule, first under the Spaniards and then under the Americans and Japanese, have given us a deep sense of inferiority. Unfortunately, the Spaniards who introduced us to Christianity also used it to control us. As Francisco points out: *"Kinasangkapan ng mga Kastila at ng kanilang alipures ang larawan ni Kristo upang mapanatili ang dayuhang kapangyarihan"* [The Spaniards and their followers exploited the image of Christ in order to maintain foreign rule].[33]

---

30. Ronald M. Green, "Theodicy," in *The Encyclopedia of Religion*, ed. Mircea Eliade and Charles J. Adams, Vol. 14 (New York: Macmillan, 1987), 436.

31. George N. Capaque, "The Problem of Evil in the Filipino Context," in *Doing Theology in the Philippines*, ed. John D. Suk (Manila: Asian Theological Seminary ; OMF Literature, 2005), 103.

32. Gaspar, *Desperately Seeking*, 110.

33. See Jose Mario C. Francisco, "Panitikan at Kristiyanismong Pilipino: Ang Nagbabagong Larawan ni Kristo," *Philippine Studies* 25 (1977), 196 (translation mine). Fortunately, as

They taught that the Christ was submissive and patient, so the *indios* should patiently bear their lot.[34] What scope does this leave for lament?

Theologians and biblical scholars

But it is not just the Spaniards and our colonizers who have contributed to the absence of lament. To some extent, so have church fathers like Augustine and Protestant Reformers like Luther and Calvin. According to Billman and Migliore, Augustine limited lament to confession of sin; Calvin was open to expressions of lament, but insisted that it should be done in a controlled and moderate manner. Luther's view was similar to Calvin's.[35] Biblical scholars have also frowned on lamentation. Westermann criticizes

> the fact that lamentation has been severed from prayer in Christian piety throughout the history of the church. In the Old Testament lamentation is an intrinsic component of prayer . . . In the Christian church, on the other hand, the lament no longer receives a hearing. This transformation took place without being discussed in the official theologies of the church. Nowhere is there a reasoned rejection of lamentation as an intrinsic component of prayer; the severing of lamentation from prayer took place without comment.[36]

In recent years some scholars have tried to redress this balance. Unfortunately, however, as I have tried to show elsewhere, some of those who have tried to promote lament have ended up diminishing its significance.[37]

Francisco also goes on to show, there were those among our people who saw in Jesus someone who regarded everyone as equal. This was a source of empowerment and prevented absolute subjugation of our spirits.

34. Ibid., 195–196.

35. Kathleen D. Billman and Daniel L. Migliore, *Rachel's Cry: Prayer of Lament and Rebirth of Hope* (Cleveland, OH: United Church Press, 1999), 73–74. Though Calvin sees Jeremiah as also a model for "protest against God," the overall emphasis is on "repentance and faith," as is true of Calvin's other expositions. See Pete Wilcox, "John Calvin's Interpretation of Lamentations," in *Great Is Thy Faithfulness?: Reading Lamentations as Sacred Scripture*, eds. Robin A Parry and Heath Thomas (Eugene, OR: Pickwick Publications, 2011), 125–130. For a helpful introduction to how the church fathers interpreted Lamentations, see Heath Thomas, "Lamentations in the Patristic Period," in *Great Is Thy Faithfulness?: Reading Lamentations as Sacred Scripture*, eds. Robin A Parry and Heath Thomas (Eugene, OR: Pickwick Publications, 2011), 113–119.

36. Claus Westermann, *Lamentations: Issues and Interpretation*, trans. Charles Muenchow (Edinburgh: T & T Clark, 1994), 81–82.

37. Federico G. Villanueva, *The "Uncertainty of a Hearing": A Study of the Sudden Change of Mood in the Psalms of Lament*, VTSup (Leiden: Brill, 2008).

This is due to a one-sided emphasis on the sudden change of mood from lament to praise in some of the psalms, along with the view that lament always moves on to or ends in praise. But while it is true that many of the psalms of lament do move on to praise, this is not the only direction in which they move. Some move in the opposite direction, from thanksgiving to lament (see Ps 9–10), or alternate between praise and lamentation (Ps 35), or end on a note of lament (Ps 12). We see that same pattern in the book of Lamentations, for after the hymnic praise of the "steadfast love of the Lord" in Lamentations 3, the rest of the chapter returns to lamentation. The whole book ends on a note of uncertainty. There is lament until the end.

Our unease with confrontation

Lastly, I think part of the reason for the absence of lament in Filipino culture has to do with the fact that by nature we prefer to avoid confrontation. We are not comfortable with tension. Culturally, we are not assertive. Rather than fight for our rights or question other people's authority, we just accept what is done. This is especially true in relation to elderly people or people in authority. I remember as a child I would remain quiet in class even when I knew the answer or had a question about the topic. We have a high respect for the elderly. If we would never question an elderly person, how much more so would we not question God. Who are we to ask, "Why?" We wonder whether it is okay to lament.

IT IS OKAY TO LAMENT

Although we, and many other Christians, struggle with the idea of lament, there are also strong grounds on which we can say that there is nothing wrong with Christians lamenting. In fact, lament has deep biblical roots.

The Bible tells us so

In the Bible we often see people asking God, "Why?" In fact, of all the interrogatives (Who? Why? When? Where? How long?) addressed to God, "Why?" is the most common.[38] Look at the following examples:

- Exodus 5:22 – Moses returned to the LORD and said, "Why, Lord, why have you brought trouble on this people? Is this why you sent me?

---

38. Samuel E. Balentine, *The Hidden God: The Hiding of the Face of God in the Old Testament* (Oxford: Oxford University Press, 1983), 118–119.

- Numbers 11:11 – He asked the LORD, "Why have you brought this trouble on your servant? What have I done to displease you that you put the burden of all these people on me?"
- Joshua 7:7 – And Joshua said, "Ah, Sovereign LORD, why did you ever bring this people across the Jordan to deliver us into the hands of the Amorites to destroy us? If only we had been content to stay on the other side of the Jordan!"
- Jeremiah 14:8–9 – You who are the hope of Israel, its Savior in times of distress, why are you like a stranger in the land, like a traveler who stays only a night? Why are you like someone taken by surprise, like a warrior powerless to save?
- Isaiah 63:17 – Why, LORD, do you make us wander from your ways and harden our hearts so we do not revere you?

Jesus is our model

Even our Lord himself uttered a lament: "My God, my God, why have you forsaken me?" (Matt 27:46). Jesus was quoting the lament in Psalm 22:1 when he uttered that cry on the cross. In doing so he not only affirmed the prayers of God's people in the OT, he also became one with them in their laments – including the prayers of lament in the book of Lamentations.

If Jesus is our model when it comes to living a life before God, then we ought also to follow his example. One of the things that Jesus demonstrated is what it means to be truly human. Though he is God, he became just like us and showed us what it means to be human followers of God. He entered our humanity by being one with us in our pain. The book of Hebrews tells us "we do not have a high priest who is unable to empathize with our weaknesses, but we have one who has been tempted in every way, just as we are – yet he did not sin" (Heb 4:15). When Jesus cried on the cross, "My God, why?" he is doing so in his humanity. And the fact that the passage in Hebrews says "he did not sin" means that expressing one's laments as Jesus did is not a sin. Nor is it a sign of weak faith. Being fully human is not a sign of weakness. In fact, the more we draw close to God, the more human we become.

Confession of sin does not silence lament

One of the reasons we do not lament, as noted above, is that we are sinners. What right do we have to question God? Maybe someone like Job had the right to lament, we may admit, since he had lived a righteous life and done nothing to deserve his suffering. But the people in the book of Lamentations are not like Job. They themselves admit that they have done wrong, that they are as filthy as can be (Lam 1:9). Yet this did not prevent them from pouring out their questions to God. Sinners may also lament in the presence of God. Of course, we know that not all questioning is acceptable to God (see Mal 2:17). But laments can be a way of coming closer to him. There are people who are serious about their relationship with God and have tried their best to be faithful to him, but some tragic experience has led them to waver in their faith. Somehow, a chasm has opened between them and God. They feel unworthy, but also hurt about what has happened to them. Lament can be the bridge to bring them back to God. The book of Lamentations shows how.

Lament empowers us

For sinners to be allowed to pour out their laments to God – that is a clear sign of mercy. For God to allow his people to stand before him and pour out their questions – that is humility. Imagine the God of the universe giving humans the right to speak their minds, let alone question him! But that is the beauty of lament. God does not view us with contempt as our colonizers did. He does not want followers who only know how to say, "Yes, yes, Lord." He sees us as covenant partners. Jesus calls us his friends, not his servants. He considers us co-workers in the vineyard (1 Cor 3:9). God is not like some of our leaders who treat us like slaves and can never be questioned. He is not like a parent who tells us to shut up whenever we begin to open our mouth. The God of the Bible allows his servants to tell him what is on their hearts. When God decided to destroy the Israelites because of their idolatry, Moses stood in the gap and reasoned with God: "Why should your anger burn against your people . . . Why should the Egyptians say, 'It was with evil intent that he brought them out, to kill them in the mountains and to wipe them off the face of the earth?'" (Exod 32:11–12).[39] In Lamentations, he allows his sinful people to pour out their hearts to him: "Why do you forsake us so long?" (Lam 5:20). And he understands the survivors of Yolanda who are still asking why God had to take their loved ones away from them.

Lament brings us closer to God

We are most open with the people we are closest with. The more intimate the relationship, the greater the vulnerability and openness. This explains why people in the Bible know how to lament. They have developed the kind of

---

39. In that story, God even allowed Moses to "win" the argument, for he changed his mind (Exod 32:14).

relationship that enabled them to be open to God. As pointed out above, one of the difficulties we have when it comes to lament is that culturally we do not question those in authority. It is hard for us to be open about what we truly feel. We would rather be silent and accept the situation. Lament feels risky. We would rather maintain a quiet and "peaceful" relationship without any conflict than be intimate and risk the relationship. But this manner of dealing with our relationship with God is not healthy in the long run. For without honesty, there is no intimacy. As one of our proverbs puts it: *Ang nagsasabi ng tapat, nagsasama ng maluwat* [the one who is honest about what she/he feels will keep the relationship intact].

What makes the book of Lamentations important for us is that it shows how a people pursued God in the most trying experience of their life. It is for those who have gone or are going through tragic experiences. Though the book was written in the light of the destruction of a city, its lessons may also be applied to experiences of tragedy on a personal and communal level.

To properly appropriate Lamentations, we need to know some backgrounds about the book.

BACKGROUND TO THE BOOK OF LAMENTATIONS

In what follows, we consider who wrote the book of Lamentations, why it was written, and how it was written.

Who the author was

Like many of the books in the Bible, the book of Lamentations does not mention its author. Traditionally, it was attributed to the prophet Jeremiah, which explains its placement after the book of Jeremiah in the Septuagint and in most modern Bibles.[40] This tradition goes back to ancient times, for the Septuagint, the Greek translation of the Hebrew Bible that dates from the second century BC, introduces Lamentations with the following words: "And it came to pass after Israel had gone into captivity, and Jerusalem was laid waste, that Jeremiah sat weeping and composed this lament over Jerusalem and said . . ."

---

40. The book appears with the five scrolls (meggiloth) in the Masoretic Text: the Song of Songs, the Book of Ruth, the Book of Lamentations, Ecclesiastes and the Book of Esther. But this does not contradict the traditional view that Jeremiah wrote the book as preserved in the Septuagint. The different ordering simply reflects the status of the early development of the book. See Johan Renkema, *Lamentations*, Historical Commentary on the Old Testament (Leuven, Belgium: Peeters, 1998), 33.

The link to Jeremiah may be a result of an interpretation of the passage in 2 Chronicles 35:25 which mentions the prophet singing laments at the death of King Josiah.[41] However, there is really no way of knowing who actually wrote the book. Some scholars hold that the chapters may have been written by different authors. In my view, the similarities between the language of the book of Jeremiah and the language of Lamentations suggest that Jeremiah could have written at least some of the book. However, we do not have to be dogmatic about this, and like Christopher Wright, I have chosen to respect the intentional anonymity of the book and will refer to the author simply as "the poet."[42]

Why the book was written

In the face of the destruction of the city of Jerusalem, the poet did not do what pastors/priests, theologians, and even ordinary Christians usually do whenever there is a disaster: he did not give advice or write a series of sermons, and he did not develop a treatise on the theology of suffering.[43] Instead, he sought to offer the people a means of expressing their grief, processing their pain, and pouring out their laments. The book of Lamentations is not a long series of sermons or theological reflections. As Brady puts it, "the book of Lamentations was written more as an expression of grief rather than a systematic theological reflection."[44] It does not seek to explain but to express. In the words of Hillers: "Lamentations was meant to serve the survivors of the catastrophe simply as an *expression* of the horror and grief they felt. People live on best after calamity, not by utterly repressing their grief and shock, but by facing it, and by measuring its dimensions."[45]

How it is structured

The poet composed five pieces of poetic literature that were structured around a Hebrew acrostic. The word "acrostic" means alphabetical, and when applied to Lamentations it means that each of the first four chapters is built around

---

41. Ibid.
42. Christopher J. H. Wright, *The Message of Lamentations: Honest to God*, Bible Speaks Today series (Nottingham: IVP, 2015), 28.
43. "It is the merit of Lamentations that it does not quickly or easily promise away the present agony. It does not encourage the remnant of Israel to take comfort in the fathers, or the Exodus, or the land, or Zion, or the line of David, or any of the old symbols of her status with God" (Delbert R. Hillers, *Lamentations*, AB [Garden City, NY: Doubleday, 1992], 5).
44. Christian M. M. Brady, *The Rabbinic Targum of Lamentations: Vindicating God* (Leiden/Boston: Brill, 2003), 8.
45. Hillers, *Lamentations*, 4.

the succession of letters in the Hebrew alphabet.[46] Verse 1 begins with the first letter of the alphabet, verse 2 with the second, and so on. It is exceedingly difficult to bring out this feature of the poetry in English, or in Tagalog, or in any other language. However, Slavitt did attempt to capture it in English. Here is the start of his translation of Lamentations 3:[47]

> Afflicted am I and beset, a man whom God in his wrath has abased.
> Abused by his rod and broken, I am driven into the darkness.
> Against me, he turned his hand, and again and again.
>
> Bones broken, wasted, I am besieged and battered.
> Bitterness is my portion and tribulation.
> Banished, I dwell in the darkest darkness like those long dead
>
> Chained so I cannot escape and walled in, I am a captive.
> Crying for help, I call out, but he will not hear my prayer.
> Crooked are all my paths, which he has blocked with boulders.

But why use the alphabet when composing a poem? If one's intention is to express the depth of one's grief, why submit to the constraints of an acrostic? There are a number of possible explanations. One is that an acrostic structure is useful when it comes to memorizing the poem.[48] Another explanation is that the acrostic structure conveys completeness. There is a Jewish saying that the law should be obeyed from *'aleph* to *taw* (a to z), that is, in its entirety. Similarly, the acrostic form conveys the idea that every grief, every lament, every question should be expressed to God. The idea is to pour out your heart to God "from a to z." The alphabet provides space for lamenting each aspect of the tragic experience.

Because of their acrostic structure, the chapters in Lamentations do not necessarily have a strong logical flow to them. That is not their primary concern. It is far more important that everything be expressed to God. This does not mean, however, that the expression of pain is boundless and chaotic, for it also has an end (z) and a form (from a to z). An acrostic is a brilliant way of expressing pain while also imposing some form on it.

---

46. The fifth chapter does not have the corresponding Hebrew letters at the beginning of each verse. But it has 22 verses corresponding to the 22 letters of the Hebrew alphabet. So there is also an attempt to follow the acrostic even in the last chapter.
47. D. R. Slavitt, *The Book of Lamentations: A Meditation and Translation* (Baltimore, MD: John Hopkins, 2001), 20. Quoted in Wright, *Message of Lamentations*, 30.
48. Norman K. Gottwald, *Studies in the Book of Lamentations* (London: SCM Press, 1962), 25.

Some psalms, including Psalm 119, are acrostics. The acrostic psalm that is most closely related to Lamentations is Psalm 9/10, for although it begins with thanksgiving it moves to lament in the second part.

THREE RESOURCES

When faced with an enormity of loss like that experienced in Yolanda or the destruction of Jerusalem, we need to draw on all our resources, both cultural and religious. When composing the book of Lamentations, the poet drew from three rich traditions, namely city laments, dirges, and laments found in the book of Psalms

City laments

As mentioned above, "city laments" were not unique to the Jews but were also composed in Mesopotamia. There are five known poetic compositions lamenting the destruction of ancient cities:

- Lamentation over the destruction of Ur
- Lamentation over the destruction of Sumer and Ur
- The Nippur lament
- The Eridu lament
- The Uruk lament

Dobbs-Allsopp compared the book of Lamentations and the Mesopotamian city laments and concluded that they are very similar. He identifies ten generic features of the Mesopotamian laments: subject and mood, structure and poetic technique, divine abandonment, assignment of responsibility, a divine agent of destruction, destruction, a weeping goddess, lamentation, restoration of the city, and return of the gods.[49] Nine of these features are present in Lamentations. The only one missing is the last one: the return of the gods.

The twin themes of Mesopotamian city laments are divine abandonment and the return of the gods.[50] In these laments, the gods always return at the end. There is a resolution. In Lamentations we certainly find the theme of abandonment, but the second theme – the return of the gods – is absent, for God never shows up in the book.

---

49. Dobbs-Allsopp, *Weep, O Daughter of Zion*, 157.
50. F. W. Dobbs-Allsopp, "Tragedy, Tradition, and Theology in the Book of Lamentations," *JSOT* 74 (1997): 32.

The positive ending of the city laments may be explained by their use during the inauguration of a rebuilt temple. But in the book of Lamentations, the temple remains in ruins. So this book has come to be associated with the commemoration of the destruction of the temple – not only of the First Temple but also of the Second Temple, and all subsequent destructions that the Jews have experienced throughout history. Every year, on the ninth of Ab (the fifth month of the year), the book of Lamentations is recited as part of the synagogue ritual on the anniversary of the destruction of the First and Second Temples. This practice makes the book of Lamentations even more relevant to occasions of mourning after disasters like Typhoon Yolanda.

Dirges and the *Dung-aw*

The poet also drew on funeral traditions. As in traditional Filipino society, people in the OT had many rituals for mourning the dead. One of these was the dirge or funeral song. Such songs are important for they announce grief and create the space people need to mourn their losses. Dirges were usually sung by women who were professional mourners (see Jer 9:17–19):

> Professional mourners were engaged not only to perform mourning in contexts of death or calamity, but to draw out the appropriate ritual response from others gathered to mourn. The lamenting of the dirge women is intended . . . to cause tears to flow from the eyes of those present, whether or not members of the assembled body are inclined to weep, for weeping in such contexts has important social functions.[51]

The characteristic cry of the dirge is the word *eikha* [how] (see comments on Lam 1:1 below).

The Ilokano people of the Philippines have preserved a form of dirge known as the *dung-aw*, which is a song of mourning ("*awit ng pagluluksa*"; in Tagalog we use the term, "pananambitan").[52] There are some similarities between a *dung-aw* and the book of Lamentations, and understanding these enriches our reading of Lamentations. For example, in both the *dung-aw* and the book of Lamentations there is an admission of sins. If the person reciting the *dung-aw* has committed a sin against the dead, she confesses this publicly.

---

51. Saul M. Olyan, *Biblical Mourning: Ritual and Social Dimensions* (Oxford: Oxford University Press, 2004), 50.
52. Lars Raymund Cortuna Ubaldo, "Dung-aw, pasyon at panagbiag: tatlong hibla ng pakasaritaan ti biag sa kasaysayang pangkalinangang Ilokano" 2003, 55.

If it was the dead person who did something wrong to her, she will also declare this and offer forgiveness.[53] Like the book of Lamentations, in which the main concern is restoration, the ultimate goal of *dung-aw* is *kaginhawaan* [well-being] for the bereaved, the dead, and those who are listening.[54] But for this to occur, grievances must be dealt with. Hence the need for reconciliation. This reconciliation extends, to some extent, to the relationship with God. Though there is surrender to the will of God in the end, this does not prevent the mourner from asking God why he took the loved one.[55]

Lament Psalms

The question "why?" is the characteristic mark of laments, which are the third resource the poet drew on when composing Lamentations.[56] We find many laments in the book of Psalms – in fact about a third of the 150 psalms are laments. This statistic shows that lament was an important part of the life of OT believers. Today the majority of our songs, if not all of them, are praise songs, but those ancient believers knew both what it meant to rejoice and also how to mourn/lament.

> One does not always sing praises and give thanks; there is also a time to grieve and lament. Alongside the happy festivals of rejoicing in the community stand the days of lamentation. When crop failure, pestilence, and danger from the enemy afflicted the people, such a day of lamentation was observed. On such occasions all the people would assemble at the sanctuary, tear their clothes, fast, weep, lament.[57]

It is not a good sign when Christians know only one type of response to everything. For the reality of life is that we all go through what Brueggemann calls the three seasons of life (a season of orientation, disorientation, and new orientation).[58] As Psalms scholar Gunkel has said, "In the alteration be-

---

53. Ibid.
54. "*una, ginhawa para sa nagdudung-aw; ikalawa, ginhawa para sa pinagdudung-awan; ikatlo, ginhawa sa mga nakikinig ng dung-aw* [first, well-being for the mourner; second, well-being for the subject of the mourning; third, well-being for those listening" (Ibid., 57).
55. Ibid.
56. For a good article on the lament psalms as an "important" resource for Christian faith and ministry, see Walter Brueggemann, "Formfulness of Grief," *Int* 31. 3 (1977): 263–275.
57. Hermann Gunkel, *The Psalms: A Form-Critical Introduction* (Philadelphia, PA: Fortress, 1967), 13.
58. Walter Brueggemann, *The Message of the Psalms: A Theological Commentary* (Minneapolis, MN: Augsburg, 1984).

tween lament and song of thanks there unrolls the whole life of the pious"[59] Sometimes we find ourselves closer to "praise;" at other times to "lament." There are also times when we are in the middle. Tragedies such as the destruction of Jerusalem and the devastation of Tacloban call for lamentation. The poet benefited from the rich tradition of lament that he had at his disposal. It shaped the communal lament at the end of the book (see Communal Lament, pp. 107–108).

LAMENTATIONS AS POETRY

All three of the poet's resources – the city laments, dirges, and lament psalms – were in poetic form. Poetry remains one of the best mediums for expressing the language of grief. It is expressive; it allows you to give a name to your experience without the exactness of mathematics. Poets thrive on ambiguity. In poetry, opposing voices are held together without resolving them. This ability makes poetry at home with life's suffering. It gives you a handle on overwhelming experiences. When we are confronted with the destruction of a city or a tragic personal experience, we need a poet. And the Jewish community is blessed to have had a poet who could make good use of the poetic devices of personification and dramatization.

Personification

As a poet, the author of the book of Lamentations made use of metaphors. He personified the city as a weeping woman. Women were traditionally associated with mourning, and by personifying the city and its inhabitants as a woman mourner, every Jew became a mourner. "She impersonates each individual survivor in Jerusalem, from infants to old men and woman."[60] Here the use of gendered language shows no disrespect to women. In Lamentations, the woman expresses what it means to be human. "When a Hebrew poet allows the woman to speak for herself, she is passionate, complex, and fully human."[61] The poet "aesthetically identifies with the suffering woman when his poem reaches the level of greatest intensity."[62] Even the

---

59. Hermann Gunkel, *Einleitung in die Psalmen die Gattungen der religiösen Lyrik Israels* (Göttingen: Vandenhoeck and Ruprecht, 1933), 284, tranlsation mine.
60. Lena-Sofia Tiemeyer, *For the Comfort of Zion the Geographical and Theological Location of Isaiah 40–55* (Leiden, Boston: Brill, 2011), 257.
61. Barbara Bakke Kaiser, "Poet as 'Female Impersonator': The Image of Daughter Zion as Speaker in Biblical Poems of Suffering," *Journal of Religion* 67.2 (1987): 165.
62. Ibid., 166.

speaker in Lamentations 3 who identifies himself as "the man" weeps (see comments in Lam 3).[63]

Personification accomplishes several things. First, it creates some space between the experience and the people. Sometimes when the experience is too close and too overwhelming, it paralyzes you. Through personification, the people can view their experience from a distance and begin the process of articulating their loss. Second, it enables you to have a multifaceted view of the situation or the tragic experience. The poet can see the situation from a distance. He can see it from the perspective of the personified woman. He can begin to understand what others feel. Third, personification also allows the poet to do things like talk to the woman.[64] The woman can speak on behalf of the poet or the people. This is important especially when you feel you do not want to say something directly to God.

Dramatized speech

One of the central issues arising from the tragic event in the book of Lamentations is the people's relationship to God. Given their view that the destruction of the city was an act of God through their enemies, how do they now approach God? Is it alright for them to mourn? Should they just accept what has happened to them as something they deserve? But what about their enemies, whom God allowed to inflict his judgment? Don't they also deserve to be punished? Granted that the people have sinned, does this mean that even the little children should be punished? If the people feel that the punishment is too much, how do they tell this to God? Shouldn't they just keep quiet and submit to whatever God has ordained? But how can a genuine relationship continue without resolving the issues confronting each of those who are party to the relationship? How can they begin to address them?

These are some of the issues/questions that arose from the Jews' experience. The solution adopted by the poet is to use dramatized speech. The following comment by Mintz is important if we are to appreciate and understand what is going on in Lamentations:

> Who speaks to whom about whom as seen from whose point
> of view? It is in the play of these questions, which defines the
> rhetorical situation of the text, that the deepest theological

---

63. Hobbins, "Zion's Plea," 169, argues that the speaker in Lamentations 3 is a woman.
64. George Lakoff and Mark Johnson, *Metaphors We Live by* (Chicago, IL: University of Chicago Press, 1980), 66.

business of Lamentations gets transacted. If we can state the theme of Lamentations as an exploration of the traumatized relations between Israel and God in the immediate aftermath of the Destruction, and if we pause to realize that as a poem Lamentations has as its medium dramatized speech and not theological statement, then we must appreciate the significance of the poem's rhetoric.[65]

In other words, we should pay close attention to who is speaking, what is being said, and to whom he or she is saying these words. We hear different speakers in the book. In the opening verses we hear the voice of a narrator. The second speaker is the personified city herself, Lady Zion, whom we encounter in the first two chapters. The third speaker describes himself as "the man." Lanahan sees a fourth speaker in chapter 4, whom he calls "bourgeois." In chapter 5 the community represents the fifth and last speaker. These different speakers are called "personas." A persona "is a creative procedure in the displacement of the poet's imagination beyond the limitations of his single viewpoint so that he may gain a manifold insight into the human experience."[66] In what follows we will try to follow the dramatized interaction between these speakers in order to understand what is happening in the book.

SUMMARY OF THE CHAPTERS

Lamentations 1

The dramatized speech in Lamentations reveals the entangled dynamics of the relationship between God and his peoples. The opening chapter begins with a cry of mourning derived from the tradition of the dirge. It is offered as a means to allow the people to mourn their terrible loss. Even as the narrator speaks, the focus zooms in on a personification – Lady Zion – who sits alone, weeping. She is compared to a widow, the epitome of vulnerability and weakness in ancient times. Some explanation is needed for what has happened, and the narrator articulates the common belief: the city has been destroyed

---

65. Alan Mintz, "The Rhetoric of Lamentations and the Representation of Catastrophe," *Prooftexts* 2 (1982): 4.

66. William F. Lanahan, "The Speaking Voice in the Book of Lamentations," *JBL* 93 (1974): 41. For an excellent discussion of the speakers in Lamentations, see Knut Heim, "The Personification of Jerusalem and the Drama of Her Bereavement in Lamentations," in *Zion, City of Our God*, eds. Richard S. Hess and Gordon J. Wenham (Grand Rapids, MI: Eerdmans, 1999), 129–169.

because of Lady Zion's many sins. However, instead of confessing her sins, Lady Zion pleads for mercy, asking the Lord to "look" at her affliction (1:9c). If it is true that the response of God's people reflects the kind of God they believe in, then God's mercy is revealed in the initial words of Lady Zion. She repeats much the same petition in verse 11c.

In the verses that follow (1:12–16) Lady Zion turns to passersby to complain that she is suffering too much. "Is any suffering like my suffering?" (1:12) she asks them. The question is a rhetorical one, to which the only possible answer is "there is none." As noted above, it is important to note who is speaking to whom. One question we need to answer here is why Lady Zion had to turn to passersby? She was crying out to the Lord in the previous verse. Why did she not continue her speech to the Lord? In her speech to the passersby, God is talked about in the third person. It is an indirect way of speaking to someone. Her speech reveals what the people felt. She is behaving a bit like Filipinos, who when they feel hurt by someone they love turn away instead of saying what they feel directly to the person concerned. Could it be that her turning to the passersby is an indication of a sense of grievance on her part? Does she feel hurt by God?[67] My own contextual reading affirms that she may indeed have been hurt. Her feelings represent what the people may have felt.

Whatever may have been the real motive of Lady Zion in turning to the passersby, it has helped her process her feelings of hurt, as can be seen in the latter part of the first chapter (vv. 18–22) where she again turns towards God. As in her first speech, she tells God of her distress and affliction. But whereas earlier she complained about God to the passersby, this time, she complains about what her enemies have done and reports this to God. Earlier, she told the passersby her grievance against God, now it is God to whom she pours out her heart.

Lamentations 2

In the second chapter, the narrator returns to the stage. His speech is similar to the speech of Lady Zion to the passersby (see comments in 2:1–8 below). But he is not talking to the passersby; he is narrating/reporting as he did before. His implicit audience is the reader or the listeners. By repeating what Lady Zion said, he is identifying with her. Like a good counsellor, he empathizes with her, feels her pain, and reiterates what she said. Those in the care

---

67. *Nagtatampo kaya siya sa Diyos?*

business have a lot to learn from this narrator. In the latter part of the chapter he not only identifies with Lady Zion but also seeks to help her even as he struggles to find language in which to express her misery (2:13). It is possible that here the poet has inserted himself into the story, unable to contain his emotions when he sees the suffering children. In any case, the poet/narrator addresses Lady Zion. His speech shows that even though like Lady Zion he may have felt grieved by the scope of God's punishment, he never let go of God. Contrary to what some scholars think,[68] Lady Zion and the poet continue to cling to God. The poet calls on her to cry out to God, to pour out her heart in the presence of the Lord (2:19). Lady Zion does this, uttering some of the most impassioned lament in the Bible (2:20–21).

Lamentations 3

In chapter 3 we hear the voice of a "man who has seen affliction" (v. 1). The description recalls the petition of Lady Zion (1:9, 11). The man testifies that he too has experienced what Lady Zion, and thus by implication every Jew, has experienced. His speech thus has an aura of authority. Finally, here is someone who had been through the same experience and has managed to move on. In his hopeless situation he remembered the Lord and he was saved. He has moved from lament to praise as he sings about the steadfast love of the Lord (3:22–23). Because of his experience, he has the right to give advice. His advice represents traditional wisdom, which basically teaches that we should submit to God come what may. We should never complain, for God has our best intentions at heart. He may bring grief, but that is not his final intention (3:33).

The man then invites the congregation to return to the Lord and repent of their sins (3:40). He leads them in a prayer of repentance. But suddenly, just after they confess their sins ("We have sinned and rebelled"), they accuse God ("you have not forgiven") (3:42). These two lines are juxtaposed in Hebrew, without any intervening "and" or "but."

What follows is a communal lament that contradicts the advice given earlier. It is not clear who is speaking or leading the community in this lament, which is comparable to the communal lament in Lamentations 5. Some argue that this part of the chapter was originally a separate composition, but even if this were the case, we have to make sense of it in its present position. It does seem to represent an anticlimax. After singing of the Lord's

---

68. Carleen Mandolfo, *Daughter Zion Talks Back to the Prophets: A Dialogic Theology of the Book of Lamentations* (Atlanta, GA: Society of Biblical Literature, 2007).

steadfast love, the people are back to lamenting. What does the dramatized speech signify at this point? Should we ignore the voice of the "man"?

In 3:49 we hear another "I" interrupting the communal lament. It is hard to know who is speaking here. Is it the "man" who spoke in the first part of the chapter? Or are we hearing another speaker, the poet perhaps, or Lady Zion? Since the chapter is unified by an extended acrostic (with each letter of the Hebrew alphabet repeated three times), and since there is no clear change of speaker, it is best to view the speaker as the same throughout the chapter. The "man" is the one leading the communal prayer as well as the "I" in the rest of the chapter. The opposing views are all brought together here to create a deliberate tension. Ongoing suffering calls for a multifaceted approach that allows for lament even while encouraging people to submit to God. For did not our Lord himself utter a cry of lament after he expressed his acceptance of the will of his Father? "Father, not as I will but as you will" (Matt 26:39) and "My God, my God, why have you forsaken me?" (Matt 27:46) go together.

Lady Zion and the "Man"

The preceding discussions have implication on the way we understand the relationship between "the man" and Lady Zion. In the past these two have been set against each other almost in some sort of a competition. Lady Zion is said to be unable to properly "reflect" on her situation. That is why we needed a "man" who can do that.[69] But as it stands, chapter 3 does not contradict what Lady Zion was saying or what she stands for. If anything, it actually reinforces her views. For what we have here is a clear example of how one was able to "overcome" his afflictions, how he was able to regain and therefore maintain his faith in God even in spite of his experience. Yet by situating the man's experience in the light of the people's continuing suffering and subsequent lament before God, the emphasis shifts from a note of certainty to a note of "uncertainty."[70] The movement is similar to Psalm 89, which having started with thanksgiving, nonetheless ended with communal lament. Thus, the man in Lamentations 3 is presented as one who continues to lament even after he had experienced an assurance from the Lord. Like Zion, he too weeps

---

69. Mintz, "Rhetoric of Lamentations," 9, tends to downplay the role of the woman in his discussion of chapter 3 and to somehow degrade lamentation itself. He says that in chapter 3, lamentation gives way to reflection in chapter 3. Only a man can do reflection; a woman can express but not reflect.

70. See Villanueva, *The Uncertainty of a Hearing*, 233–242, for further discussion.

(3:49). The portrayal of the man in chapter 3 represents the reality of life amidst continuing suffering.

Lamentations 4

The capacity to embrace ambiguity and tension enables the next speaker to continue. Chapter 4 presents an eye-witness account, written in the third person. There is no direct petition to God or prayer in this chapter; it is simply a recollection of the fall of Jerusalem. This time, the emphasis is on the seriousness of the situation the people have found themselves in. We get the sense that they have reached rock bottom. Yet it is precisely at their lowest point that they start to see a glimmer of hope. "Your punishment will end, Daughter Zion" (4:22), says the speaker.

Lamentations 5

In the last chapter, we hear the people praying. The whole chapter is a communal lament and the only extended prayer in the whole book. It is also the most direct in terms of their speech/prayer to God. We have heard cries to him earlier in the book, but they were brief and not fully developed. Here in Lamentations 5 we have a prayer with 22 verses representing the complete Hebrew alphabet. Many of the speeches in the previous chapters do mention God, but often he was talked about in the third person. Now at last the people finally become direct in their speech to God. It took four chapters before they were able to do this. Maybe like us, they needed to "beat around the bush" before they could tell God what they really wanted to say. If anything, the last chapter is the fulfilment of longing, albeit only a partial fulfilment. For even though they as a community were able to pour out their hearts to God, they never received any response from God. Everyone has said their piece, except God. The only voice missing is God's.

WHERE IS GOD IN LAMENTATIONS?

The question "Where is God in Lamentations" is not a new one. It has a long history, dating back to ancient times. The Jews themselves contemplated it, and so did the prophets. In fact, the latter part of the book of Isaiah (Isa 40–55) includes a response to Lamentations. Wright draws our attention to this in his commentary:[71]

---

71. Wright, *Message of Lamentations*, 45.

- Five times Zion moans that there is no one to comfort her . . .
  The prophet announces double comfort from God, and returns
  to the theme again and again (Isa 40:1–2; 49:13; 51:3, 12, 19;
  52:9; 54:11)
- Lady Zion grieves for the loss and fate of her children . . . The
  prophet foresees their return and multiplication (Isa 49:17–
  18, 20–22).
- The besieged citizens of Jerusalem watched in vain for a nation to
  save them (4:17). The watchmen in the ruins of the city will rejoice
  they see YHWH coming to do just that (Isa 52:8).
- The roads to Jerusalem were deserted, with all the joy of pilgrims
  gone (1:4; 5:15). The prophet sees the returning exiles coming with
  joy once more to Zion (Isa 51:11).
- Lamentations ends with Zion feeling forgotten and forsaken, under
  God's rejection and anger (5:20, 22). The prophet acknowledges
  their precise words (Isa 49:14), and that they had indeed been true
  – but only for 'a brief moment' (Isa 54:6–8).

The comforter would come. God would come. This is an important message to remember. But that came later. In Lamentations, God has decided not
to speak. For to speak would be torture. There is no speech, no words, no
encouragement that will suffice to answer the loss of a child swept away by
flood waters. Silence is the only thing that is needed . . . and tears.

Later Jewish writers, writing roughly a thousand years after the fall of
Jerusalem to Babylon, produced a midrash (an ancient commentary) on the
biblical book of Lamentations, which also mourned all subsequent destructions of Jerusalem. In *Lamentations Rabbati*, it is not the tears of the woman
but the tears of God that are highlighted. In its attempt to encourage the
Jewish people, it interprets the book of Lamentations as God's lament over
the destruction of Jerusalem and the suffering he himself has inflicted upon
his people. *Lamentations Rabbati* seeks to show that God was with them, crying out not only for them but with them: "Just as a human king mourns the
death of his son, God mourns the destruction of Jerusalem" [Lam Rabbati
67–68, 203–204]. It presents God, not Jeremiah or the people of Israel, as
uttering the plaintive words of Jeremiah 8:23: "Oh, that my head were water,

my eyes a fount of tears! Then would I weep day and night for the slain of my poor people" [Lam Rabbati 138, 140].[72]

IMPORTANCE OF LAMENTATIONS IN THE ASIAN CONTEXT

Lamentations' emphasis on tears, lament, uncertainty, mourning, and suffering resonates with our experience in Asia today. These are the main themes of many theologies that are being produced here. From Kitamori's *Theology of the Pain of God* to Nirmal's *dalit* theology; from the *minjung* theology of Korea to the Philippines' theology of struggle, "what brings much of the Third World together is a sense of pain."[73] It is not the prosperity gospel but the theology of suffering, of lament, that marks the theology of Asia. But this theology has a specific focus; it is the kind of theology of suffering that makes engagement between God and his people possible. In Lamentations we encounter a God who shares our pain simply by allowing his people to express to him all their questions, hurts, doubts, and pain.

Lamentations is perhaps best understood by expressing our own laments to God. The following prayer of lament by Karl Gaspar, written in response to the devastation of Tacloban and surrounding areas, represents an attempt to engage God in the way that the people in Lamentations did:[74]

> We believe in you as the Great Provider (*Makagagahum nga Tig-tagana*), our dear God. But what sort of "gifts and blessings" have you provided Your people? Yes, you have provided us with the gift of our lives, our ancestors and families, our wisdom and talents. Yes, you have provided us the blessings of nature, of the sky, sea and land from which we are able to sustain ourselves in this delicate planet . . .
>
> But what Your right hand provides, the left hand taketh away! These past few years, in the whole planet – and specifically in the islands that constitute our native land – calamity after calamity has struck and in their wake, thousands of lives are lost and millions of properties destroyed. In the aftermath, there is pain, trauma, suffering and grief. Children lose their

---

72. Shaye J. D. Cohen, "The Destruction: From Scripture to Midrash," *Prooftexts* 2 (1982): 34.
73. John Parratt, ed., *An Introduction to Third World Theologies* (Cambridge, UK: Cambridge University Press, 2004), 11. Kazo Kitamori, *Theology of the Pain of God* (Richmond, VA: John Knox Press, 1965).
74. Gaspar, *Desperately Seeking*, 220–221. Permission granted by author.

parents, grandparents lose their grandchildren, entire neigh-
borhoods and communities are fragmented, farms and fishing
grounds are dissipated and the people are turned scavengers in
order to survive the wreckage of the disasters. And deep into the
psyche of the survivors are deep traumatic wounds that will take
years to heal.

Where is your love and compassion when you seem to be
absent in this landscape; as if you turn into a parent who abandons Your children and disappear from their midst?

Since viewing the extent of the devastation, we cannot help
but echo the questions in the hearts of the survivors: why did
this calamity happen? Why did it happen to us? What kind of
punishment is this if we are supposed to be punished? What sins
have we committed if this is some kind of punishment? What
are you trying to tell us? What lies ahead for our children and
their children?

As we listen to the people's stories about what they underwent, we not only hear the words but the sound of tears fall-
ing on their cheeks. No matter how we try to remain stoic in
the face of these personal tragedies, we, too, shed our own tears
as we seek to empathize with them in these moments of grief.
We witness to their sense of frustration for Your abandonment,
even as we intuit that these are like children's expression of being
neglected by their parents who ignored them in their hour of
need . . .

LAMENTATIONS 1

Lamentations 1 starts with a great cry, "*eikha*" (v. 1). It is very important that we note this, for crying is slowly fading away from our society. There used to be much weeping at funerals; these days there is karaoke singing. In Sta. Barbara in Pangasinan province I recently heard a band, complete with drums and electric guitars, playing at a funeral. What a contrast to the funeral my *lolo* (grandfather) had many years ago! Unfortunately, in many parts of the world traditional mourning rites are being replaced by "celebrations of life." There is no place left for loud lament, but only for quiet or silent weeping.[1]

Such a development is especially harmful in a culture that tends to ignore its problems and likes to sing *Tawanan mo ang iyong problema* [Laugh at your problems – a popular song in the Philippines]. Some Christians even contribute to the problem by teaching that we ought always to rejoice, even in times of loss. One Christian group was even singing praise songs at the height of the destruction wrought by Typhoon Yolanda! When asked how they are, some Christians immediately recite Bible verses like Romans 8:28: "in all things God works for the good of those who love him." But though this is true it does not prohibit us from admitting that life is sometimes difficult. The book of Psalms acknowledges this, asking, "How can we sing the songs of the Lord while in a foreign land?" (Ps 137:4). How can we sing praise songs when we are surrounded by dead bodies, including the bodies of family members, when everything we ever gathered and built has been destroyed, and we have nowhere to go? The poet who wrote Psalm 137 was "exquisitely aware that in the wake of the destruction, the poetic discourse about Jerusalem . . . must change from *praise to lament*" (emphasis mine).[2] Even the Apostle Paul, the man who commanded us to "rejoice in the Lord always," also tells us to "mourn with those who mourn" (Rom 12:15).

By giving prominence to mourning, Lamentations 1 provides us with the necessary space for grieving our loss. For some of us even the word "loss" is too soft a word to describe what we have gone through. Karl Gaspar relates the story of the death of Cyrille Joy:

---

1. See James MacLynn Wilce, *Crying Shame Metaculture, Modernity, and the Exaggerated Death of Lament* (Malden, MA/Oxford: Wiley-Blackwell, 2009).
2. Adele Berlin, "Psalms and the Literature of Exile: Psalms 137, 44, 69 and 78," in *The Book of Psalms: Composition and Reception*, ed. Peter W. Flint et al. (Leiden/Boston: Brill, 2005), 71.

Bernadette Tenegra was clinging on to a piece of wood along with a daughter Cyrille Joy. Knowing that her chances of survival was slim and that her mother could also perish if she did not save herself, she told her mother: "Save yourself Mama, for the sake of my two other siblings who may have survived."[3]

One of the most difficult questions is the one we do not want to utter: How can God allow such a thing to happen? In a strongly fate-centered culture, we readily submit to the "will of God." So do those from traditional Chinese culture who submit to "the will of heaven."[4] But there are also those among us who harbor a sense of grievance [*sama ng loob*] against God as a result of what they have experienced. Some no longer go to church or have turned their backs on God.

How do we deal with our sense that God has let us down? Leslie Allen sees the book of Lamentations as one way of doing so.[5] As we will see, Lamentations 1 deals with grieving in a way that is both honest and culturally sensitive – and that fits in well with our own Filipino culture (See Lament as a Pouring Out of Grievance to God, pp. 52–53).

We hear two speakers in Lamentations 1. The first is the narrator who mourns the suffering of his people as he describes their experience. He does not speak as a detached observer but as someone who shares the pain and suffering of his people. As a poet, he not only expresses his own grief but also enables others to mourn through his composition. The second speaker is Lady Zion, the personification of the city and all its inhabitants. The reader is invited to share in her pain as she mourns her loss. Her voice breaks in to interrupt the narrator at certain points (vv. 9, 11). She is given space to pour out her heart in verses 12–16. At the end of the chapter, we again hear her crying out to the Lord (vv. 20–22). Thus the chapter begins and ends with a cry.

1:1–2 THE IMPORTANCE OF MOURNING

Faced with a tragedy like the destruction of Jerusalem or the devastation of the city of Tacloban by Typhoon Yolanda, you need to dig deep into your cultural resources to cope with the situation. That was what the poet did when he started his composition with the word *eikha*. This Hebrew word is usually

---

3. Gaspar, *Desperately Seeking*, 55.
4. Lee, "Lamentations," 232.
5. Allen, *Liturgy of Grief*, 20–21.

rendered in English as "how," but this translation utterly fails to capture the depth of emotion in the original Hebrew. Allen's translation, "How terrible . . ."[6] is far better.

Eikha was the cry that marked the start of a funeral dirge. It is similar to David's cry as he began his great lament for Saul: "How the mighty have fallen!" (2 Sam 1:19). It is a cry wrung from the heart, like the "*ay*" with which our own Ilocano dirges begin: "*Ay anacco, anacco apay yaonayen*" [Oh, my child, my child, how unfortunate it is!] or "*Ay ipapasco daguitoy nga leddaang*" [Oh! Let me express all these griefs and sorrows].[7] Such dirges express "elemental grief, melancholy, and lamentation for the death of a beloved one."[8]

It is no accident that the word *eikha* begins with *aleph* (represented by the sign '), the first letter of the Hebrew alphabet. One of the difficulties in the face of great tragedy is how we even begin to mourn. What can we say? In such a situation, we can begin with the very first letter of our language, whether *eikha* or *ay*, and proceed to tell our griefs from a to z. (For more on the use of acrostic structures in Lamentations, see the Introduction.)

Personification

One of the difficulties in the early stages of a loss is our incapacity to describe what we are going through. We grope around in the dark, filled with fear of the unknown future. The terrors we have endured and the images that infiltrate our sleep continue to haunt us. It helps if we can give a name to them. This capacity to give a name to what we are going through, to attach some shape to it, is a crucial step towards healing.

Both poets and the biblical writers knew this long before psychologists became aware of it. We see this in their use of metaphorical devices to capture, or put a name to, what we are feeling. For example, we can understand what someone means when they say that they are "on an emotional roller coaster." That metaphor helps us to understand that the person is experiencing a succession of emotional ups and downs. In the psalms, David used metaphors to describe his own experience: "the waters have come up to my neck. I sink in the miry depths, where there is no foothold" (Ps 69:1–2). Overcome by fear,

---

6. Ibid., 6.
7. This is taken from a a *dung-aw* from Santa, Ilocos Sur. See Presentacion Lahoz, "The Dung-Aw, The Ilocano Dirge," *Ilocos Review* 2 (1970): 66–67. Ilocano is one of the major languages in the Philippines. The *dung-aw* is pre-Hispanic (Ibid., 63).
8. Berlin, "Psalms and the Literature of Exile," 71.

he lamented: "I am in the midst of lions . . . men whose teeth are spears and arrows, whose tongues are sharp swords" (57:4).

Poetry speaks to us in times of crisis when we feel overwhelmed. That is why when Typhoon Yolanda devastated Tacloban, poets, songwriters, and artists came together to compose poems or songs expressing our people's experience.[9] So it is not surprising that the author of Lamentations turned to poetry when confronted by overwhelming loss, for "poetry is perhaps the ideal medium for expressing the emotions of grief"[10] and poets are "good observers of human emotions."[11]

One of the problems the poet who composed Lamentations faced was how to represent the suffering of a whole people, rather than just the suffering of an individual. The solution he arrived at was to use the figure of speech known as personification to depict the city and its inhabitants as a woman sitting alone, weeping (vv. 1–2).[12] In personification "an inanimate object or an abstract concept is spoken of as though it were endowed with life or with human attributes or feelings."[13] The value of personification is that it establishes some distance between the people and their experience, thus enabling them to gain some perspective on it. It also "makes use of one of the best source domains we have – ourselves. In personifying nonhumans as humans, we can begin to understand them a little better."[14]

So in Lamentations 1, the poet uses personification to help the people mourn their loss. He represents the city as a woman because in Judah, as in the Philippines,[15] dirges were composed by women, who were the primary mourners at funerals.[16] At a time when "the destruction is a national death and all Judeans are mourners,"[17] everyone can identify with this woman and

---

9. Rosana B. Golez and Joel P. Garduce, *Surges: Outpourings in Haiyan/Yolanda's Wake* (Makati, Philippines, 2013).
10. John Archer, *The Nature of Grief: The Evolution and Psychology of Reactions to Loss* (New York: Routledge, 1999), 35.
11. Ibid., 12. Here Archer quotes Shand.
12. "The solution undertaken by the authors of Lamentations was to transfer to the collective the attributes of individual experience and to view the nation as a whole in the aspect of a single individual; simply put: personification" (Mintz, "Rhetoric of Lamentations," 1.)
13. M. H. Abrams and Geoffrey Galt Harpham, *A Glossary of Literary Terms*, 10th ed. (Boston, MA: Wadsworth, 2012), 132.
14. Zoltán Kövecses and Réka Benczes, *Metaphor: A Practical Introduction* (Oxford: Oxford University Press, 2010), 39.
15. Lahoz, "The Dung-Aw, The Ilocano Dirge," 62, 72.
16. Saul M. Olyan, *Biblical Mourning: Ritual and Social Dimensions*, 50.
17. Adele Berlin, "On Writing a Commentary on Lamentations," in *Lamentations in Ancient and Contemporary Cultural Contexts*, eds. Nancy C. Lee and Carleen Mandolfo (Atlanta, GA: Society of Biblical Literature, 2008), 9.

become a mourner. This was the people's response to the catastrophe that has come upon them.

Mourning rituals

In OT times, there were many rituals associated with mourning. In addition to singing a dirge, mourners would tear their garments, weep, fast, wail, toss ashes or dust on their heads, and sit on the ground.[18] That is exactly how the poet describes the woman in Lamentations (v. 1). Her posture is part of the ritual of mourning. But whereas there would normally be a crowd of mourners, this woman sits "alone." We do not normally see this at a funeral. Why is the woman sitting alone? It is because "there is no one to comfort her" (v. 2). Her pitiable condition is reinforced by the statement that she who "was once great among the nations" has now become "like a widow" (v. 1). Widows were among the most vulnerable groups in ancient society. They lacked any legal protector and could be "abused with impunity."[19]

In verse 2, there is a reference to Lady Zion weeping "bitterly . . . at night." Why "at night"? Because it is usually during the night that we are alone. During the day there are people around and things to do to keep us busy. But at night there are no distractions, and we lie awake, exhausted but unable to sleep. That is when the weeping comes, and how bitter are those tears!

I remember talking to a mother who had lost her loved ones in Tacloban. She pointed to the high water tank where her husband was swept away by the rushing water. Two of her four children also drowned. Unable to support her two surviving children, she had sent them to Manila to stay with their aunt while she stayed on alone in Tacloban. During the day, she tried to work. But in the dark loneliness of the night, tears born of unbearable pain would flow. No words could express her agony. Only tears.

Lady Zion, too, has tears "on her cheeks" (v. 2). Usually, tears run quickly down our cheeks and dry, but Lady Zion's tears remain frozen in place as the poet focuses our attention on them. Like the mother in Tacloban, Lady Zion has no words to utter. Only the tears on her cheeks testify to the depth of her pain.

Unfortunately, we are often in too much of a hurry to pay attention to the tears on our sister's or brother's cheeks. We simply try to stop their flow, and urge the mourner to contain their grief. We are too quick to offer advice

18. Olyan, *Biblical Mourning*, 13.
19. Mintz, "Rhetoric of Lamentations," 3.

instead of noticing, listening, and just being present with them in their suffering.[20] The poet is demonstrating what it means to be with people who are suffering.

The importance of *pakikiramay* (being one with others)

Having someone to accompany you in your grief is a gift. Having no one is a curse. The tears on Lady Zion's cheeks continue to flow not only because of her terrible loss but also because "there is no one to comfort her" (2:2). Her "lovers" and "friends" have all turned their backs on her. Here these "lovers" and "friends" are Israel's allies, for in ancient times, mourning with those who mourn had a political dimension.[21] When a king died, his allies and vassals were expected to send representatives to join the court in mourning. This was what David did when the king of the Ammonites died. The members of his delegation were referred to as "comforters" (2 Sam 10:3, ESV). "In addition to sending an embassy of comforters to the court of the dead king, a ruler, upon learning of the death of his treaty partner, might fast, weep and lament, declaring a public fast to mark his ally's death."[22]

On a communal level as well as on a personal level, having someone to comfort you when you are suffering is one of the most important resources in times of mourning. This "comfort" means, among other things, weeping with the one who is bereaved, or in the case of a disaster, being one with the people in their mourning.[23] This was what Job's friends did: "They began to weep aloud, and they tore their robes and sprinkled dust on their heads. They sat on the ground with him" (Job 2:12–13). In Filipino, we call this *pakikiramay*, the act of sharing in the grief of those we care about. Many Filipinos are prepared to fly home from abroad to attend the funeral of a loved one. We consider it a debt of gratitude (*utang na loob*), which can never be repaid, when someone shows *pakikiramay* to us in our times of loss.

Unfortunately, Lady Zion did not receive any comfort. Five times in chapter 1 the poet says, "there is no one to comfort her" (vv. 2, 9, 16, 17, 21). The repetition underscores the people's "misery and isolation."[24] The situation is similar in Tacloban. In the early days following the devastation

---

20. Even in our reading of the book of Lamentations and of this commentary we tend to hurry.
21. Helene P. Foley, *Female Acts in Greek Tragedy* (Princeton, NJ: Princeton University Press, 2001), 19–55.
22. Olyan, *Biblical Mourning*, 49.
23. Ibid., 46–49.
24. Ibid., 88. Olyan makes this comment in regard to Psalm 35, but it also applies to Lamentations 1:2.

of Tacloban, when the streets were full of bodies and many were desperately searching for loved ones or for anything to eat, the government was not there to "comfort" them. Instead, the government representatives tasked with delivering the much needed help were more concerned with politicking than with helping the people. Instead of showing sympathy, they made enemies. Meanwhile, the people suffered; they felt betrayed, abandoned, like Lady Zion. Such insensitivity, such obsession with power, blinds people to the needs of those who are dying before their eyes.

1:3–4, 6–7 THE AGONY OF EXILE AND THE DESOLATION OF THE CITY OF JERUSALEM

Throughout this chapter the poet models what it means to be a comforter. Having wept for the loss of his people (vv. 1–2), he describes how hard their experience had been as he narrates Judah's experience of exile (v. 3). In doing so, he also demonstrates what it means to process our pain. Telling the story is part of the journey towards restoration.

As if exile itself were not difficult enough, the narrator adds that Judah has gone into exile "in affliction and harsh labor" (v. 3, my translation).[25] The additional detail adds to the depth of their suffering. The scope of the suffering too is broadened, for it is no longer just the city that is affected (v. 1) but "Judah" (v. 3). Thus the personified "city" represents not just Jerusalem but also the whole of Judah and its inhabitants.

The narrator reports that Judah "dwells among the nations." The word translated "dwells" comes from the same verb used in verse 1, where it was translated "sits." Unlike Lady Zion who sits "alone," Judah sits "among the nations." Yet, even though Judah is not alone, she is unable to find rest. The last line of verse 3 further underscores the difficulty of their experience: Their enemies attacked "in the midst of her distress." Vulnerable and weak, the people of Judah have become passive objects of their enemies' actions.

The account in 2 Kings 25 provides the details. The Babylonian army had surrounded the city of Jerusalem and set up a siege. Nothing could be brought into the city, and as a result "there was no food for the people to eat"

---

25. The NIV translates this verse as "After affliction and harsh labor, Judah has gone into exile" (v. 3). The word translated "after" comes from the Hebrew preposition *min*, which can mean "from," "out of," "because of," "in," or "into." I prefer the last option. For more information, see Robert B. Salters, *Lamentations. A Critical and Exegetical Commentary* (London/New York: T & T Clark, 2010), 42–43. See also Nahum M. Sarna, "Interchange of the Prepositions *Beth* and *Min* in Biblical Hebrew," *JBL* 78 (1959): 310–316.

(2 Kgs 25:3). When the city's defenses crumbled, their enemies entered the city, hunting down those who tried to escape, killing them, and burning the city. Any survivors were carried off into exile (2 Kgs 25:11). The few who were allowed to remain in the land were the poorest of the poor.

The experience presented in verse 3 is similar to the experience of the victims of Typhoon Yolanda. "Long before Yolanda, these islands' citizens have experienced a reality of poverty and destitution. Way back from the era of their ancestors . . . the Warays have constantly faced hunger, deprivation and powerlessness."[26] They were forced to live near the sea because they had nowhere else to go. The disaster came on a distressed people, and the strongest winds in recorded history bulldozed the city and its surrounding area. Tacloban was left looking like a war zone. Even its road was destroyed.

After these words about the exile, the poet again turns his attention to the city, which he here calls "Zion" (v. 4). The name Zion can be used to refer to Judah or to the entire people of Israel.[27] It originally referred to a "fortress in Jerusalem during the period just before David captured the city from the Jebusites."[28] Later, this area was called Mount Zion. This was where Solomon built the temple. Eventually, "'Zion' came to refer to Jerusalem itself, that is, to the entire temple city."[29] Finally, "Zion, like Jerusalem, came to refer to the people of Israel and not just their temple mountain and city" (Isa 51:16).[30] In Lamentations 1:4, however, "Zion" refers to the city of Jerusalem and more specifically to the temple.

The psalmist described Zion as "the city of our God . . . beautiful in its loftiness, the joy of the whole earth" (Ps 48:1–2; see also Lam 2:15). The temple choir proclaimed that even if the earth were to crumble, the city of Jerusalem would be secure (Ps 46). But now this place of beauty and strength has become lonely, weak, and pitiable. She who was once a queen "has become a slave" (Lam 1:1). Joy has turned to lament as "the roads to Zion mourn" (v. 4). The reference to the roads reflects the close link between the people and their city. Roads are so mundane that we hardly notice them. But here the inanimate is endowed with life, only to offer a cry. When stones start speaking, people are in great trouble (see Luke 19:40). Where the psalmist

---

26. Gaspar, *Desperately Seeking*, 14. The "Warays" are a subgroup of the people in the Visayas region of the Philippines.
27. W. Harold Mare, "Zion," *ABD* 6:1096 says "Zion is 'a very common appellative for Jerusalem and God's people.'"
28. Jon D. Levenson, "Zion Traditions," *ABD* 6:1098.
29. Ibid.
30. Ibid.

used to say, "I rejoiced with those who said to me, 'Let us go to the house of the LORD'" (Ps 122:1), now "no one comes to her appointed festivals" (Lam 1:4). Even prominent places like the gates where important decisions were made are now "desolate." As a result, the "priests groan" and the "young women grieve."

In verse 6a the poet continues to lament what has been lost: "All the splendor has departed from Daughter Zion." The only thing they can do is remember "all the treasures that were hers in days of old" (v. 7). Like the Israelites in the desert who longed to return to their life in Egypt the survivors of Jerusalem remember the precious possessions that were once theirs. But whereas a return remains a possibility for those exiled, there is no such possibility for the survivors left in Jerusalem. Their previous life is gone.

The emphasis on "splendor" and "treasures" reveals that it was not only the poor in Jerusalem who suffered. Even Zion's "princes" (the leaders or officials of the people) struggle to survive. They have become "like deer that find no pasture" (v. 6b). Like the Jews in exile, they cannot find rest (v. 3). When disaster strikes, there is no distinction between rich or poor. We saw this with Typhoon Yolanda, for many of those who died in the aftermath were "residents of big, concrete houses."[31] Not even the mayor of Tacloban was spared. His own family were "swamped by the waves in their seaside house and survived only by the skin of their teeth, helped by two trusted security guards who staked their lives for them."[32]

In Jerusalem, the princes who were supposed to be strong have fled "in weakness . . . before the pursuer" (v. 6c).

1:5, 8–9B MEANING-MAKING

Surrounded by rubble and destruction, the people naturally ask, "Why has this happened to us?" One of the needs of the survivors of any disaster "is to find meaning in what they underwent; the more devastating the catastrophe, the greater is the desire to be able to acquire a semblance of the meaning of that terrifying experience."[33] The answer given to the question, "why has this happened to us?" is part of what is called "meaning-making" or "theologizing." In verse 5, the narrator does his own "theologizing" as he tries to make

---

31. Report from the Institute for the Study of Asian Church and Culture (ISACC), a faith-based organization that helped in the rehabilitation work in Tacloban.
32. Ibid.
33. Gaspar, *Desperately Seeking*, 102.

sense of what happened. He too cannot help but wonder why all of these disasters have come upon his people.

The poet's interpretation of events reflects the common theology of OT and even NT times. When someone became sick or was struck by tragedy, people assumed it was because they had done something wrong. So when Jesus' disciples saw a man who was blind from birth, they attributed his disability either to his own sin or his parents' sin (John 9:1–2). Though not limited to this view, the poet believes it is because of Lady Zion's "many sins" (Lam 1:5) that their suffering has come upon them. Elsewhere, Nehemiah confessed that the people failed to obey the Lord: "They were disobedient and rebelled against you; they turned their backs on your law" (Neh 9:26). As a result, God gave them over to their enemies who triumphed over them: "So you delivered them into the hands of their enemies, who oppressed them" (Neh 9:27). Deuteronomy 28 promised that "The LORD will make you the head, not the tail. If you pay attention to the commands of the LORD your God that I give you this day and carefully follow them, you will always be at the top, never at the bottom" (Deut 28:13). But the people failed, as the poet confesses: "Her foes have become the head" (Lam 1:5, ESV). This is because of the Lord's action in view of the people's many sins.

The traditional Asian view is the same. In times of disaster, Indonesians would offer sacrifices to appease the gods. Similarly, after Typhoon Yolanda struck Tacloban and surrounding areas, the prayer, *Patawarin mo kami* [Forgive us] was posted everywhere, including on the ship that was driven by the storm surge into streets. This short prayer reveals at least two theological beliefs: First, that God caused the disaster, and secondly, that it happened because of their sins.

Verse 8 could be literally translated as "Jerusalem sinned a sin." This is not a reference to some specific sin but is a way of saying that things had gone seriously wrong in Jerusalem. As a result, the city "has become unclean."[34] The word translated "unclean" is similar to the word used in Leviticus 18:19 to refer to a menstruating woman, who was ritually unclean. However, the uncleanness referred to in Lamentations 1 is not merely ritual; it also has a

---

34. The association of being unclean with menstruation is further supported by the "filthiness" (*tumah*) in 1:9a. For alternative interpretations of the words in 1:8, see Adele Berlin, *Lamentations: A Commentary* (Louisville, KY: Westminster John Knox Press, 2002), 53–54.

strong moral element (see v. 5).[35] This is also the case in Isaiah 64:6, where the prophet confesses that "all of us have become like one who is unclean."

Verses 5 and 8–9b represent the first prayer of confession in Lamentations. Later in verse 18 we will find another confession. Such prayers become common after the exile (see Ezra 9:6–15; Neh 1:5–11; 9:5–37; Dan 9:5–19). But the later prayers are more elaborate and extended in their confession of and emphasis on sin. For example, look at Daniel 9:5–7: "we have sinned and done wrong. We have been wicked and have rebelled; we have turned away from your commands and laws. We have not listened to your servants the prophets, who spoke in your name to our kings, our princes and our ancestors, and to all the people of the land. Lord, you are righteous." Compared to that prayer, the confessions in Lamentations 1 are very brief indeed.

The confession in Lamentations 1:5 is cut short by the mention of the suffering of the children: "Her children have gone into exile, captive before the foe." The word translated "children" comes from the Hebrew word, *olal,* which refers to infants and very young children, often in the context of violence done to them. The word occurs about twenty times in the OT, most often in the book of Lamentations. Given how short this book is, the number of references to children is significant.

1:9C–17 BEYOND CONFESSION

The implied complaint as reflected in the narrator's description of the suffering of the children is characteristic of the lament psalms. The people are confessing their sins, yet at the same time they are being honest about what they feel about their situation. There is an acknowledgment of the justice of God's action (see v. 18), but this does not prevent them from voicing their complaints about the punishment.

We find this same juxtaposition of confession and complaint in other passages in the OT. For example, in the prayer of lament in Isaiah 63:7–64:12 the people ask: "Why, LORD, do you make us wander from your ways and harden our hearts so we do not revere you?" (63:17). Yet a few verses later, we hear one of the most moving confessions in the Bible: "We have all

---

35. For more on the distinction between ritual and moral uncleanness, see Jonathan Klawans, *Impurity and Sin in Ancient Judaism* (Oxford/New York: Oxford University Press, 2000), 21–42.

become like one who is unclean, and all our righteous deeds are like a polluted garment" (64:6; see also Jer 14:7–9).[36]

1:9c Juxtaposition of confession and lament

In Lamentations 1, confession (vv. 5ab, 8–9ab) and lament (vv. 5c, 9c) go together.[37] This is true elsewhere in the book too (see comment in Lam 3:42). This juxtaposition teaches us that though the theology of retribution is correct, this does not prevent us from expressing to God what we truly feel. Confession does not silence the voice of protest. Even in confession the door to lament and remonstration is never shut. We confess our sin while at the same time being honest about what we truly feel about our experiences of tragedy or loss.

This point is important, for there is a tendency to silence questioning and lamenting, even in the face of the most tragic events. The rush towards resolution and the pressure to make it appear that things are normal can lead to the marginalization of the families of victims. After 300 Korean students drowned when a ferry sank, the families of the victims complained that not only had the government not done enough but that they were actively discouraged from protesting about the official negligence that contributed to the disaster. When there is no place for lament and honest expression of feelings, confession loses its meaning. In such circumstances, prayers of confession may sound pious, but they are not real. Unless the questions of the heart are dealt with, there will not be genuine restoration.

The wonderful thing about our God is that he does not stifle the voices of those who suffer, even when complaints are hurled at him (see vv. 12–16). The poet is allowed to express his grievance (see v. 5 above). Lady Zion's plea reflects God's mercy. After the confession of sin in verses 8–9ab, she interrupts the narrator: "Look, LORD, on my affliction, for the enemy has triumphed" (v. 9c). Lady Zion could have uttered her own prayer of confession following the narrator's confession. Instead, her first words are an impassioned plea for mercy. Like the Lamenter earlier who started with a cry of mourning, not

---

36. Jeremiah, too, both confesses the people's sins and complains to God: "Though our iniquities testify against us, act, O LORD, for your name's sake; for our backslidings are many; we have sinned against you. O you hope of Israel, its savior in time of trouble, why should you be like a stranger in the land, like a traveler who turns aside to tarry for a night? Why should you be like a man confused, like a mighty warrior who cannot save? Yet you, O LORD, are in the midst of us, and we are called by your name; do not leave us" (Jer 14:7–9).

37. In the OT, "protest in the teeth of God's justice and confession of sin go hand in hand" (Hobbins, "Zion's Plea," 160, n. 16).

with any accusation of sinfulness, so Lady Zion begins with a cry for mercy. It is significant that both the narrator and Lady Zion begins with a cry and not with a confession of sin.[38]

If it is true that the response of the people to God mirrors the character of God,[39] then the first words of Lady Zion reveal a God who is compassionate. The concern for mercy goes before repentance.[40] Though Lady Zion admits she has sinned and that God is justified in his actions (see v. 18), this does not prevent her from asking God to look at her and see her affliction.

1:10–11 Rape and hunger

The petition for God to "look" (*raah*) at Zion's affliction becomes even more urgent as the narrator reports how Zion "saw (*raah*) pagan nations enter her sanctuary" (v. 10). In line with the acrostic form of chapter one, which conveys a sense of completeness, every aspect of the suffering experienced by the people is being aired. The poet mourns that Judah's friends and lovers have turned into enemies (v. 2). The suffering within and outside Jerusalem is portrayed in verses 3 and 4. The loss of all that was precious is lamented in verses 6 and 7.

In verse 10, the poet speaks of what happened when the enemy broke through the city's defenses. Using the language of rape, he describes how they "laid hands on all her treasures." The word "treasures" is a "cipher for rape, based on the correspondence between genitals and inner sanctuary in the metaphor of Zion as both woman and city."[41] This is implied in the personification of the city as a woman, which according to Bergant, is

> derived from the relationship between inhabitants and their city of origin. They are the ones who perceive the city as the mother from whom they come and upon whom they depend for survival. The history of cities is often told through the use of sexual metaphors. Cities are established and defended by men; their

---

38. Miriam J. Bier, "'Perhaps There Is Hope': Reading Lamentations as a Polyphony of Pain, Penitence, and Protest," Thesis for the Degree of Doctor of Philosophy (University of Otago, Dunedin, New Zealand, 2012), 139.
39. Walther Zimmerli, *Old Testament Theology in Outline* (Edinburgh: T & T Clark, 1978), 141, writes: "And it is also true that in the 'response' God expects from those he addresses God himself can be recognized as in a mirror."
40. Incidentally, Pope Francis declared this year (2015–2016) as the "Year of Mercy."
41. Bier, "Perhaps There Is Hope," 145.

land is fertile and productive or barren and worthless; when their walls are penetrated, they are said to have been violated.[42]

The language of rape is reinforced by the statement that the enemy has entered "her sanctuary" (v. 10). Like the flood forcing its way into the houses in Tacloban, so her enemies "entered" Jerusalem. They even entered God's holy place – something he had said would not happen (see Pss 46, 48). The shock the people felt must have been profound. "Not only are temple treasures seized, but in the metaphorical context, there is a groping violation of Zion's person."[43]

Although in verse 10 we hear the voice of the narrator again after a brief interruption by Lady Zion, the shift to the second person at the end of that verse brings back the voice of Lady Zion as she speaks of "those *you* had forbidden to enter your assembly." The mingling of the voices of the narrator and Lady Zion reveals the unity of their views and emotions. One can also detect indirect questioning – Why has this happened? Why have you allowed this to happen? Didn't you say that enemies would not enter your sanctuary? (see comments on vv. 12–16).

In verse 11, we are confronted with another tragic result of disaster or war – hunger. The ancient lament for the city of Ur includes the words: "Ur – its weak and (its) strong perished through hunger."[44] The poet shares the same experience as he reports: "All her people groan as they search for bread" (v. 11). Earlier, it was the priests who groaned as the city lay desolate (v. 4). In verse 8, the personified Jerusalem groans over her shame. Here, the people groan because of hunger. They would give everything they have in exchange for food (v. 11).

In the days immediately following the devastation of Tacloban there were reports of looting. While some of this was done by outsiders and criminals, much of the so-called "looting" was done by the desperate inhabitants of the city. No relief supplies were coming in and the people had no recourse but to take food from grocery stores. Later, many of them felt ashamed that they had been "stealing," as this was something they would never have done in the ordinary course of life. Maybe that was how Lady Zion felt when she cried out on behalf of her children: "Look, LORD, and consider, for I am despised" (v. 11c). Like her earlier petition (v. 9c), this prayer is very short.

---

42. Dianne Bergant, "'êkāh: A Gasp of Desperation (Lamentations 1:1)," *Int* 67, (2013), 150.
43. Bier, "Perhaps There Is Hope," 145.
44. Kramer, "Lamentation," line 227.

This is the second time that Lady Zion interrupts the narrator. From this point on, she will be the main speaker in this chapter.

1:12–16 Lady Zion pours out her heart to the passersby

In her brief prayer in verse 11c, Lady Zion calls on God to "see . . . and look." Then she immediately turns to the passersby, calling on them to "look and see" (v. 12).[45] This repetition of the words (which the ESV translation brings out very clearly) establish a link between the two verses.

It is interesting that in Lamentations 1 the narrator never addresses God directly or complains to him directly. Instead, the personified Lady Zion is the one who talks to God. We in Asia, particularly Filipinos, are familiar with this indirect way of communicating. Few of us share the American preference for direct speech. We prefer to take an indirect route and use various channels to convey our concerns. Some may complain that we beat around the bush, but that is our way of doing things.[46] This is especially true when we are dealing with the elderly or people in authority. How much more when we are communicating with God?

In the book of Psalms, we see the psalmist doing something similar. In Psalm 10, for example, the psalmist has his enemy say, "God will never notice; he covers his face and never sees" (10:11). As the next verses (12–13) reveal, however, it is actually the psalmist who feels that God "never sees." Similarly, in Lamentations 1, the fact that the poet is unable to utter a direct petition to God probably indicates that he has a sense of grievance. Thus, he puts words into mouth of Lady Zion. But even she is unable to express her complaints directly to God. She instead utters them to passersby. These passersby could be actual people or, like Lady Zion, poetic creations that serve as a channel through which Lady Zion can pour out her complaint.

Lady Zion's turning to passersby also reminds us of the importance of sharing our pain with someone as we process our grief. It is very important for those who have been through some traumatic experience to share their story and verbalize their feelings. We are taught to bring everything to God. But what if we feel that it is God who has hurt us? How do we deal with this? It would be ideal if we could directly tell God about what we feel. But culturally, it may be helpful to share what we are going through with another

---

45. The opening words of v. 12 are obscure in the original Hebrew. They can be interpreted as an imperative, a question, or a wish. For a fuller discussion of this, see Salters, *Lamentations*, 73.
46. See Maggay, *Pahiwatig*.

person or a group whom we can trust and who understand that it is alright to feel hurt by God. One young photographer shared his feelings with me in this way. When he saw what had happened to Tacloban, he felt that God had abandoned the city and was angry that God could allow such a thing to happen. Although he was a member of the worship team in his church, for some Sundays he found it difficult to go to church. In Filipino, we would say, *nagtampo siya sa Diyos* [he has a grievance against God]. Whether he was correct in his theology or not is not important at that point. What was important was for me to listen to him and affirm the validity of his feelings, just as the author of the book of Lamentations did as he heard the laments of his people.

Lady Zion tries to process her pain by sharing her feelings about the treatment she has received from God. Her question, "Is any suffering like my suffering?" (v. 12) is rhetorical. The expected answer is "It has no equal; there is nothing like it." She then goes on to describe how the Lord has afflicted her. God is the subject of the main verbs in verses 13–15. She speaks about God's "fierce anger" (v. 12), describing it as a fire that she can feel in her bones. We usually think of answers to our prayers coming "from on high." But in Zion's case, what came to her from on high is not an answer to prayer but the consuming fire of divine judgment (compare Lev 10:1–3). In his fierce anger, God became like an enemy who "spread a net for my feet and turned me back" (v. 13). The Hebrew word for "spread" (*paras*) is the same as that used in v. 10 to speak of the enemy who "laid" (*paras*) hands on all of Zion's treasures" (v. 10).

Lady Zion relates how "my sins have been bound into a yoke, by his hands they were woven together" (v. 14).[47] Earlier, the narrator acknowledged that it was because of "her many sins" that the Lord had afflicted her (v. 5). Here Lady Zion herself admits her transgressions. But as in the earlier confessions, she does not focus on her sins. Instead, she calls attention to what God has done with them. He has caused her sins to be bound into a yoke.[48] Now that she is trapped with her feet caught in his net (v. 13), God sets the yoke of her transgressions on her neck.[49] With her feet entangled,

---

47. The verb translated, "woven together," literally means "intertwined" or "fastened."

48. The exact verb here is unclear. It may be either "to watch" or "to bind" (Salters, *Lamentations*, 79). Whichever word is correct, the meaning is clearly something unpleasant, for Yahweh is punishing Jerusalem.

49. It is possible that the subject of the verb *'alah* is the transgressions, in which case the verse is saying that their transgressions have gone up to their neck (compare Ps 69:1).

and her neck bowed under the weight of this yoke, her strength fails. Weak and helpless, she is unable to withstand her enemies. Earlier, she cried out for help to the Lord "for the enemy has triumphed" (v. 11). But here she tells the passersby that it is the Lord himself who "has given me into the hands of those I cannot withstand" (v. 14).

In verse 15 Lady Zion states what the preceding verses have already made obvious – God is against her. God has "rejected all the warriors in my midst," crushed "my young men," and "trampled Virgin Daughter Judah." The first two lines are parallel: the first speaks of "my warriors"; the second of "my young men." There is a progression in terms of God's action against Zion and its people. The Lord rejects them, then he crushes them, and finally he tramples them down. The change from "young men" to "virgin daughter" makes the emotion even more vivid. The word "daughter" is a term of endearment, and so the phrase could be translated "Dear Zion" or even "Sweet Little Zion."[50] The connotations of the word increase our perception of the element of cruelty in God's actions. This idea will be developed further in Lamentations 2.

"This is why I weep" (v. 16a), Lady Zion tells the passersby. The word "this" is actually plural in Hebrew, and so the phrase could be translated, "For these things I weep" (ESV), referring to everything Lady Zion has been speaking about to the passersby (vv. 12–15). Earlier, the narrator reported that Lady Zion was weeping bitterly (v. 2). Now we hear from Lady Zion herself: "my eyes overflow with tears."[51]

Why do her tears flow? Again she says it is because "no one is near to comfort me, no one to restore my spirit" (v. 16b). The absence of a comforter was first mentioned in verse 2. The same point is made four more times in this chapter. Look at the verses in the ESV translation:

- "she has none to comfort her" (v. 2)
- "she has no comforter" (v. 9)
- "a comforter is far from me" (v. 16)
- "there is none to comfort her" (v. 17)
- "there is no one to comfort me" (v. 21)

Of the five occurrences of the phrase, verse 16 is the only one presented as direct speech, the one where Lady Zion herself is speaking. In all the other cases, the words are those of the narrator. The phrase in verse 16 is also the

---

50. Berlin, *Lamentations*, 12.
51. The Hebrew of v. 16 literally reads, "my eyes, my eyes flow with water."

only one to include a verb; in the Hebrew, all the others are verbless constructions. This signals the importance of this verse. It can be translated as: "for a comforter has become far (or turned away) from me."

In verse 2, the expected comforters were her allies. But in verse 16, Lady Zion is speaking of a different comforter, one who could "restore my spirit" (v. 16b). Who is this if not the Lord, for he is the only comforter who could truly restore Zion (see Lam 5:21). Lady Zion weeps because she feels that the Lord himself, the one who can truly restore her spirit, has turned away from her.

The narrator interrupts at this stage to remind us of the heartbreaking appearance of Lady Zion as she stretches out her arms to God in desperation (v. 17a). Counselors and those involved in the ministry of caring can learn a great deal from the way the narrator/poet notices the details of Lady Zion's words and posture. He sees the tears on her cheeks (v. 2). He notices her outstretched hand. He acknowledges her utter desolation and does not try to minimize it or argue it away. He confirms what she has declared: "there is no one to comfort her" (v. 17a).

The "outstretched hand" is not only an appeal for help; it is also a prayer. The psalmist adopts the same posture: "I stretch out my hands to you; my soul thirsts for you like a parched land" (Ps 143:6). Like Lady Zion, the psalmist is faint and pleads for God's mercy (Ps 143:4). But whereas God "commands his steadfast love" to the psalmist (Ps 42:8); such was not the case for Lady Zion: "the LORD has commanded against Jacob that his neighbors should be his foes" (Lam 1:17b). This supports the explanation given above of why Lady Zion is weeping – not only have her allies turned away from her, even her God has turned against her. As will be seen in the other chapters of Lamentations, the ultimate desire of the poet as well as the people is for God to see them (3:49–50) and for them to be restored to God (5:21). Elsewhere, God promised the house of Israel that he would "command his angels concerning you" (Ps 91:11). But here he does the opposite, commanding the enemy to invade the city. As a result, they have become "a filthy thing" (Lam 1:17c). They are to be shunned like someone who is ritually unclean or, even worse, they are to be destroyed.

1:18–22 NEVER LETTING GO OF GOD

In Lamentations 1, Lady Zion moves between praying to God and addressing passersby:

- Prayer to God (vv. 9, 11)
  - Address to the passersby/people (vv. 12–16)
  - Address to the passersby/people (v. 18)
- Prayer to God (vv. 19–22)

This structure shows that Lady Zion's addresses begin and end with God. She may lament how God has treated her but she never let go of him. Like the psalmist she may cry out, "Why have you forsaken me?" but she also continues to call him "my God" (Ps 22:1). Understandably, she may try looking for help elsewhere, but in the end she realizes it is only God who can help her. Though she views God as the one who has allowed the suffering, he is also the healer. The prayer the young girl uttered as the waters came flooding in captures this very well: *"Jesus, tama na po"* (Jesus, please enough) (see Introduction). The ultimate goal in Lamentations is restoration to God. But before there could be restoration, the people had to process their sense of grievance (see Lament as a Pouring Out of Grievance to God, pp. 52–53).

It is remarkable that even after all that Lady Zion had said about God to the passersby (vv. 12–16) she still maintains that the Lord is justified in his actions against her. She declares: "The LORD is righteous, yet I rebelled against his command" (v. 18a). This is another way of saying, "Lord, you are right; I am wrong" (see also Neh 9:33; Dan 9:7). Maybe her pouring out of her heart to the passersby has helped.[52] Somehow, as she unloaded her ill-feelings about God to others, her sense of hurt was lessened.

Though one can still sense an element of complaint as Lady Zion turns from the Lord to the people in verse 18b, there is a noticeable change. She addresses the people: "Listen, all you peoples; look on my suffering. My young men and young woman have gone into exile." The repetition of the same word for "suffering" (*mak'ob*) used in verse 12 indicates that Lady Zion is addressing the same group (the passersby). But whereas before she went on to give details of her suffering, this later speech leads her to God. If earlier, her speech to God was cut short as Lady Zion turned to the people, here it is the other way around. In verses 19 and 20 she turns her attention to God.

---

52. Some argue that Lady Zion is not showing a renewed commitment to pursue God but is putting herself in the right and God in the wrong. For example, see Mandolfo, *Daughter Zion*. Hobbins, "Zion's Plea," 161, strongly rejects this view, arguing that if there is one thing Lady Zion desires it is that the Lord will see her. It is important that we be careful how we handle issues like this so that we do not become like divorce lawyers who are more interested in breaking a relationship than mending it.

Lady Zion acknowledges that human help is unreliable: "I called to my allies but they betrayed me" (v. 19). The verb "called" is often used with reference to prayer (see, for example, Ps 34:6). By using this verb, Lady Zion prepares for her actual prayer, which follows in Lamentations 1:20–22. This prayer begins with a petition that God "see" her distressful situation (v. 20) and "hear" her groaning (v. 21) and ends with a prayer against her enemies (v. 22).

Lady Zion's cry "See, LORD, how distressed I am!" (v. 20) reminds us of her earlier pleas in verses 9 and 11.[53] Her persistence in prayer shows her continuing faith that, unlike her allies, the Lord will answer her (see Lam 5). Even when she feels God has turned away from her (v. 16), she continues to cling on to him. Like the Canaanite woman who never gave up even when Jesus told her that what he was offering was not for her (Matt 15:21–28), Lady Zion continues to come to God: "Hear how I groan; there is none to comfort me" (v. 21, RSV). When viewed in the light of her earlier speech and the rest of the book of Lamentations, her faith is remarkable indeed!

The second part of her prayer is directed against her enemies. There is a significant repetition of the verb "to hear" in verse 21a (RSV): "Hear, how I groan . . . All my enemies have heard of my trouble." God has to hear her because her enemies have already heard about her.[54] It is one thing to be heard by God and quite another thing to be heard by one's enemies. The latter leads to further agony as the enemies "rejoice" over her suffering. Lady Zion attributes this rejoicing to God's own action: "they rejoice at what you have done" (v. 21b). She could have uttered a complaint against God here. Instead, she utters a prayer against her enemies.

If earlier, she reported to the passersby what God has done to her, here she tells God what her enemies have done to her and asks God to punish them as he did her (vv. 21c–22b).[55] The journey towards restoration has begun.

---

53. There is also a stylistic parallel with vv. 11c and 12. There we noted the use of "see and look" and "look and see." Here in vv. 18–21 there is a similar inversion of "hear and see" and "see and hear."

54. The NIV translates the first word in the Hebrew as third person plural: "they heard" ("People have heard my groaning"), following the MT. But the LXX has the imperative form "Hear!" though also in the plural form. I think the latter reading is preferable since: (1) there is no explicit subject; (2) the context supports this reading, for v. 21 is a continuation of the petition in v. 20; and (3) it is likely that the reading in the MT might have been occasioned by the *sham'u* in the next line. See also Hillers, *Lamentations*, 77 and Salters, *Lamentations*, 100–101.

55. The last line of v. 21 is difficult to interpret. A literal translation of the Hebrew is "you brought the day you have announced, that they may be like me." It is probably best to interpret "the day" as referring to the day of wrath inflicted on Lady Zion, and to link their

The basis for her prayer against her enemies is the justice of God. In Hebrew, the petition, "deal with them as you have dealt with me" (v. 22) recalls what happened to the children of Lady Zion who have gone to exile (v. 5), for the verb for "deal" is *'alal* and the word for "children" is *'olal*. What her enemies have done to her is as wrong as her own actions, and so she prays that their sins too be punished. But in the end, she can only cite her pitiable condition as the motivation for God to answer her: "My groans are many and my heart is faint" (v. 22c).[56]

---

becoming "like me" with the prayer of imprecation in the next verse.
56. The word "many" (v. 22) and the word "great" (v. 1) come from the same Hebrew word (*rab*), forming an inclusio.

LAMENT AS A POURING OUT
OF GRIEVANCE TO GOD

Lament should be understood within the context of an intimate relationship. This is true even in our relationship with God.

I once asked my mother-in-law to name her best friend. Immediately, she said, "God." God can be our best friend. As Jesus told his disciples, "I no longer call you servants . . . Instead, I have called you friends" (John 15:15). But as in any close relationship, there will be occasions when one member of the relationship is hurt by the other. This is true especially during difficult times, when expectations are high. When my mother-in-law went through a difficult time, I asked her if she had been praying about it. Her reply: "I have already been doing that for a long time, but there was no response." I sensed a certain grievance, a feeling of hurt [*sama ng loob*]. She expected her "best friend" to resolve the problem but he seemed not to be listening.

A pastor has told me about a similar experience when he asked one of his members why he was no longer coming to church. The man replied, "I have grievance against God." He related how he had tried to live a life of faithfulness to God, and yet in spite of this his business had gone bankrupt. Meanwhile, his brother who never went to church had been successful.

We encounter a similar sentiment in the book of Psalms. The psalmist too was losing his faith in God because he saw that those who were arrogant were far more successful than he was, even though he had lived a faithful life (Ps 73:1–3). But the psalmist was able to regain his bearings. He tells us that one reason he did not lose his faith in God was his experience when he "entered the sanctuary of God" (Ps 73:17). Often, when we experience feelings of hurt, we move away. And there are times when we need to have some space to express our hurt feelings. But we need to be careful, or our drifting away from God will be final. That is why the pastor told the man who no longer went to church, why don't you tell God your grievance? The man was surprised, "You mean, it is alright for me to tell God my hurt?" Yes, the pastor affirmed. In fact, the Bible not only welcomes the expression of lament, it even encourages it.

But some may ask, who are we to question God? What right have we to have hurt feelings [*sama ng loob*] against God? We are all sinners. I think this is where the book of Lamentations becomes relevant. Unlike Job who did no wrong but suffered, the people in Lamentations admit that they are sinners. They see the connection between their wrongdoing and their present suffering (see, for example, Lam 1:6, 8–9, 18). And yet one can also sense a feeling of grievance on their part because they perceive their punishment as excessive. Lady Zion tells the passersby, "Is any suffering like my suffering that was inflicted on me, that the LORD brought on me in the day of his fierce anger?" (1:12; cf. 18). Even though she knew she had sinned, this did not prevent her from feeling hurt by God. The poet himself broke into tears when he saw the children and infants fainting in the streets (2:11). It is the sight of the suffering of children and those who are innocent that caused the feeling of hurt. Why do these children have to suffer? Why should a young child be found walking barefoot among the ruins of Tacloban, looking for his parents who were taken by Typhoon Yolanda? Why?

Some of us can ignore such suffering and submit to the will of God. Those who have a strong belief in fate find it easier to accept that everything that happens is the will of Heaven. Some Christians recite verses like, "All things work together for good to them that love God." But not all Christians find it easy to accept everything, especially tragedy. One survey conducted among the survivors of Typhoon Yolanda showed that a high percentage of those who exhibited post-traumatic stress were members of churches and faith-based organizations. It is likely that one factor in their stress was their expectation that God would save their loved ones and friends, but he did not. The conflict between their faith and the realities they faced created a situation of what is known as "internal dissonance."[1]

Even the people in the Bible showed signs of being hurt by God. The psalmist says, "I say to God my Rock, 'Why have you forgotten me?'" (Ps 42:9). Isaiah 10:5–19 is "clearly a response to a sense of grievance at what was regarded as excessive suffering, for which the human enemy was blamed rather than God."[2] We discern the same feeling in the book of Lamentations.

It is worth noting that Lady Zion does not express her grievance directly to God. Instead, she turns to the passersby. She needs someone else to help her process her pain. So did the poet who expressed his grief through this lament put into the mouth of Lady Zion.

The good thing is that they did not keep what they felt within them. Instead, they poured it out to the Lord. And that is the exhortation of the poet in Lamentations – pour out your heart to God (2:19). This is important, for when a sense of hurt (*tampo*) is not dealt with, it becomes bitterness (*hinanakit*), then anger (*galit*), and finally wrath (*poot*). We too are being invited to pour out our hearts to God. Some of us may need someone to journey with us, someone to whom we can talk about what we have experienced. This is part of the process of healing so that our heart can be restored to God once again. For is he not our best friend?

---

1. Melba P. Maggay, "Haiyan Challenge" (Philippines: Institute for Studies in Asian Church and Culture, December 1, 2013), 5.
2. Allen, *Liturgy of Grief*, 20.

LAMENTATIONS 2

In 2010, Typhoon Juan devastated parts of the Philippines. In its aftermath, aid workers sought to help children by encouraging them to gather in focus group discussions (FGD) and talk about their feelings. In one such meeting, a girl from a barrio in Isabela expressed her feelings of hurt towards God. The other children immediately censored her, saying, *"Ay . . . bad na magtampo kay God"* [It is wrong to have bad feelings towards God]. The girl shut down and never said anything else in the group.[1]

The children's response reflects the view that it is wrong to have bad feelings about God. But it is important to be able to express our feelings. We all need to find a safe place where we can pour out our hurt and our questions. In chapter 1 we saw that Lady Zion had no one to whom she could safely do this. All her friends and loved ones had either deserted her or been torn away from her. There was no one to comfort her. So she turned to the passersby and voiced her feelings about God to them.

But simply expressing our feelings is not enough. We need to hear that what we are doing is not wrong, that such emotions are valid and not necessarily sinful. We need a community who will not immediately judge us but will understand what we are going through. The theologian Nicholas Wolsterstorff recognized this when he lost his 25-year-old son in a mountain-climbing accident:

> Please: Don't say it's not really so bad. Because it is . . . If you think your task as comforter is to tell me that really, all things considered, it's not so bad, you do not sit with me in my grief but place yourself off in the distance away from me. Over there, you are of no help. What I need to hear from you is that you recognize how painful it is. I need to hear from you that you are with me in my desperation. To comfort me, you have to come close. Come sit beside me on my mourning bench.[2]

In Lamentations 2, the narrator does just that. In the previous chapter, Lady Zion expressed her hurt at what God has done (1:12–16); in chapter 2,

---

1. This story is related by Violeta Villaroman-Bautista, "Spirituality and Resilience in Disaster Situations: Sources of Life and Strength in Critical Times," in *Walking with God: Christian Spirituality in the Asian Context*, eds. Charles R. Ringma and Karen Hollenbeck-Wuest (Manila: Asian Theological Seminary and OMF Literature, 2014), 172.
2. Nicholas Wolterstorff, *Lament for a Son* (Grand Rapids, MI: Eerdmans, 1987), 34.

the narrator affirms her feelings. He shares her pain (vv. 1–8) and weeps with her (vv. 11–12), even as he struggles to find the right words to comfort her (v. 13). For someone to talk about God as Lady Zion does could be seen as tantamount to blasphemy. But far from rebuking her, the narrator expresses the same sentiments. His words at the start of Lamentations 2 are similar to those of Lady Zion in chapter 1.

Once again, we are shown a model for dealing with people who are struggling emotionally, including those who have a grievance against God. The narrator demonstrates what it means to listen, allowing others to pour out their hearts, and by sitting with them to feel what they feel and identify with their struggles. As we too journey with the suffering and the hurting, we will soon realize, like the narrator, how very little we can do for them. Any words of comfort ring hollow. Oh how much we long to help them, but how little we have to offer! Yet as we try to come alongside and care for them, we learn to cling to our faith in a God whom we believe still cares. Though the narrator shares Lady Zion's feelings of hurt against God, like her, he never let go of God. He knows that as in any human relationship, the only way to resolve one's feelings of hurt before God is to go to him. That is why the narrator exhorts Lady Zion to "pour out your heart like water in the presence of the Lord" (2:19). He is inviting Lady Zion to go on the same journey as the psalmist: "When I tried to understand all this, it troubled me deeply . . . till I entered the sanctuary of God" (Ps 73:16–17).

But before we can come to God, we need to process our hurt. We need someone who will listen to us without judging us. We need someone or some group to affirm and validate what we feel or what we are going through. How much we need such a community, especially during times of disaster! Such people are a gift from God. They bring us closer to God, even when we feel God has hurt us. By being with us, by feeling our pain, they remind us there is a God who understands us and knows the pain we are suffering.

2:1–8 THE NARRATOR IDENTIFIES WITH LADY ZION

It is not easy to read the opening verses of Lamentations 2. They are disturbing. As a Christian commentator, I find it difficult to write about them. It is not that the words are difficult to interpret. The verses are quite straightforward. What makes it challenging is the way in which God is presented. We think of God as loving, gracious, and kind. We love to name our blessings, not our woes. Hymns exhort us to count our blessings and "name them one by one." We enjoy echoing the psalmist, "Praise the LORD, my soul, and forget not all his benefits" (Ps 103:2). He then lists all the good things the Lord has done (e.g. forgiving our sins, redeeming our lives). But in Lamentations 2, what we have are the opposite – the terrible things God has done. It is these that the narrator names one by one:

- "The Lord hurled down the splendor of Israel" (v. 1)
- "Without pity the Lord has swallowed up all the dwellings of Jacob" (v. 2)
- The Lord has "cut off every horn of Israel" (v. 3)
- "He has slain all who were pleasing to the eye" (v. 4)
- He has "swallowed up Israel . . ." and "destroyed her strongholds" (v. 5)
- "He has multiplied mourning and lamentation for Daughter Judah" (v. 5)
- "He has laid waste his dwelling like a garden" and "has destroyed his place of meeting" (v. 6)
- "The Lord has rejected his altar and abandoned his sanctuary" (v. 7)

Most painful of all, God has done all these quite deliberately: "The Lord determined to tear down the wall around Daughter Zion" (v. 8). God is angry. The word for anger comes up repeatedly in the chapter. He burns in anger against his people. And his anger wreaks widespread destruction. The word *kol*, which means "all' or "every," is repeated four times in verses 2–4. There is no attempt to sanitize what God has done. He is said to have acted "without pity" (vv. 2, 17, 21). Rather than being his people's savior, God has become "like an enemy" (vv. 4–5). The verb, "to swallow," is repeated four times: in verse 2 God swallowed their dwellings, in verse 5 he swallowed Israel and swallowed its palaces, and in verse 8 we are told that he "did not withhold his hands from destroying" (literally, "swallowing"). Like the waters that swallowed Tacloban, God swallowed them up.

How are we to read Lamentations 2:1–8? What is the narrator doing in these verses? We may find it easier to answer this question if we compare these verses with Lady Zion's speech in 1:12–16. When we do this, we see that there are significant similarities between them in terms of the words used, the view of God, and the overall perspective.

Similarities between 1:12–16 and 2:1–8

1:12–16 Lady Zion pours out her heart to the passersby	2:1–8 The narrator identifies with Lady Zion
"*in the day* of *his* fierce *anger*" (1:12)	"*in the day of his anger*" (2:1; see also vv. 21–22)
"*from on high* he sent fire" (1:13)	"*from heaven* to earth" he has hurled down the splendor of Israel (2:1)
"from on high he sent *fire*" (1:13)	"He has burned in Jacob like a flaming *fire*" (2:3)
The Lord acts like an enemy: "He spread a net for my feet" (1:13)	"Like an *enemy* he has strung his bow" (2:3)
"He has given me into the hands of those I cannot withstand" (1:14)	"He has withdrawn his right hand at the approach of the enemy" (2:3)
"The Lord has rejected all the warriors in my midst; he has summoned an army . . . to crush my young men" (1:15)	"he has cut off every horn of Israel" (2:3)
"This is why I weep . . . for a comforter has gone far from me" (1:16, my translation)	"he has not remembered his footstool" (2:1); "The Lord has rejected his altar and abandoned his sanctuary" (2:7)

1) The phrase, "in the day of his anger" occurs in both passages (2:1), with the addition of the description, "fierce" in Lamentations 1:12. The theme of divine anger features prominently in Lamentations 2. The word for anger (*af*) is repeated four times in the first section (vv. 1–8): twice in verse 1, at the beginning and end of the verse, and again in verses 3 and 6. Two other Hebrew words translated "wrath" in the NIV are also used – *ebrah* (v. 2) and *hemah* (v. 4). God is angry indeed: "He has burned in Jacob like a flaming fire" (v. 3; compare 1:17).

2) There is a movement downwards. God has sent fire from heaven upon Lady Zion (1:13), and he has hurled the splendor of Israel down "from heaven to earth" (2:1).

3) The word "fire" is used in both chapters as a symbol of destruction and punishment (1:13; 2:3).

4) God acts like an enemy. In the same way that her "enemy laid hands on all her treasures" (1:10), so the Lord has "spread a net for my feet" (1:13). The words translated "laid" and "spread" in verses 10 and 13, respectively, come from the same Hebrew word (*paras*). The repetition draws a deliberate link between the enemy and God. What is implied in Lamentations 1 becomes explicit in chapter 2 as the narrator describes the Lord as being "like an enemy" who has "strung his bow" (2:4, 5).

5) As proof that God indeed has become like an enemy to them, Lady Zion declares: "He has given me into the hands of those I cannot withstand" (1:14). The narrator confirms this: "He has withdrawn his right hand at the approach of the enemy" (2:3).

6) The Lord has rejected the strong men of Israel ("warriors" in 1:15; "horn" in 2:3).

7) In both passages God's presence is the most important element in their situation. There are many reasons why Lady Zion weeps. But one of the primary reasons is that "a comforter has gone far away from her" (1:16, my translation). The comforter she is referring to here is none other than the Lord himself. To be rejected by her friends and allies is painful enough. To be trampled on by her enemies is agonizing. But what makes all of this doubly painful is that God himself, the one who "restores her spirit" has abandoned her (see comments on 1:16). Only those who are close to God can experience this feeling of being hurt by him.[3]

The narrator shares the same sentiment. For him, the most important thing is the presence of God among his people. That is why the first things he mentions is God's hurling down of the "splendor of Israel" (2:1). Splendor is a word that can refer to all the things that make people proud, including beauty, ornaments, great buildings, and so forth. However, in Lamentations 2:1 the "splendor of Israel" refers to the presence of God. We can be sure of this because of two other words used in this sentence, namely "footstool" and "Zion."

---

3. See "Lament as a Pouring Out of Grievance to God," 52–53.

The OT writers recognized that God's actual dwelling was in heaven, but they referred to the earthly temple where his presence was believed to reside as his footstool. We see this in Psalm 132:7, where the psalmist says, "Let us go to his dwelling place; let us worship at his footstool" (see also 1 Chr 28:2).

"Zion" was often used to refer to the city of Jerusalem and all the people of the land (see on 1:4). But specifically, it was the place where the temple was located on the hill that was known as Mount Zion, and thus it could also be used to refer to the temple itself.[4] That is what is happening here. By choosing to use the word "Zion," the narrator highlights the importance of worship and the presence of God. For Israel, God's presence, symbolized by the temple, was the most valuable thing in the entire nation. Moses would not trade God's presence for anything else. During the exodus, he declared that the Israelites' journey should come to an end if the Lord would not to allow his divine presence to go with them: "If your Presence does not go with us, do not send us up from here" (Exod 33:15).

At Christmas, Christians often refer to Jesus as "Immanuel," which means "God with us" (Matt 1:23). We value God's presence, for as the Apostle Paul declares, "If God is for us, who can be against us" (Rom 8:31). But what if God is against us? Who can then be for us? If God is against us, our situation is truly tragic.

The narrator in Lamentations values the presence of God highly and so he mourns because God has rejected his footstool (v. 1) and "rejected his altar and abandoned his sanctuary" (v. 7). Notice that the things associated with the presence of God are mentioned at the beginning and end of the first section (vv. 1 and 7). What grieves the narrator to the heart is that God actually chose to do all these things (v. 8; compare 1:16). Twice, the narrator says that the Lord has caused the city and its inhabitants to lament: "He has multiplied mourning and lamentation" (v. 5), and he has "made ramparts and walls lament" (v. 8). We understand the reasons for his lamentation: it is because, the glory of the Lord has departed and God has rejected his people.

---

4. This usage involves the figure of speech known as metonymy, in which something is referred to by mentioning something else that is associated with it, for example, here, Zion is used as a metonymy of the entire city of Jerusalem. The word choice is not random, but reflects what aspect of the situation the writer wants to focus on. Metonymy "allows us to focus more specifically on certain aspects of what is being referred to" (Lakoff and Johnson, *Metaphors We Live By*, 37). Thus, in focusing on Zion, the poet highlights the importance of worship, since it is the place where the temple is built. The belief in the inviolability of Zion because it is the abode of the Most High may also be at play here. For more on metonymy in general, see the chapter on this topic in Lakoff and Johnson, *Metaphors We Live By*.

The purpose of the similarities

What do the similarities discussed above show us? The close link between the dramatized speech of Lady Zion (1:12–16) and that of the narrator (2:1–8) conveys the latter's identification with the experience of Lady Zion. The switch in the speaker from Lady Zion (Lam 1) to the narrator (Lam 2) could have led to a change of perspective. But the way in which the sentiments of Lady Zion are sustained in chapter 2 suggests a sharing of viewpoint, a way of identifying, of being one with. From the reader's point of view, this can be understood as the narrator's way of comforting Lady Zion. He accepts and participates with her (*pakikiramay*) in her feelings and views. He thus validates the views about God that Lady Zion expressed to the passersby. Rather than preaching to her, correcting her, or even rebuking her; he "paraphrases" what she had said in his own words. He identifies with her tears, feels her pain, cries over her loss. Bergant's observation is to the point:

> The narration does not rush prematurely to relief, rejuvenation, and restoration. Instead, it draws out the profound desolation experienced by those who survive tragedy, those who are often plunged into despair because of what they were forced to witness and must now live with or live without for the rest of their days. One might say that in sparing none of the details of Daughter Zion's heartbreaking adversity, the narrator is showing the city respect, allowing her the freedom to give full expression to her grief, desperation, and even despair.[5]

Pastorally, Lamentations 2:1–8 teaches us about the importance of being one with those who are suffering. Often, we are too quick to come up with an explanation and "defend" God from those who express their hurt feelings about God. Worse, we indirectly rebuke those who express negative feelings about God. One mother who had lost everything in Tacloban was told by well-meaning Christians that God had a plan for her. She angrily responded, "It's good for them they know the plan of God for me!" The narrator shows us the proper approach. It is in trying to be in the shoes of our brother or sister who is going through pain that we become comforters. To comfort means to weep with those who weep; to see things from their perspective.

Theologically, these verses reveal the vulnerability of God. In Lamentations 2, God is the one in the dock as it were. He is talked about in the third

---

5. Bergant, "'êkāh," 150.

person. And the things that are said about him are hostile. His actions, and thus God himself, are said to be "without pity" (vv. 2, 21). God is presented as the "perpetrator," the one who caused the destruction of Jerusalem. Yet the remarkable thing is that God did not prevent Lady Zion from sharing her views with others, nor did he intervene to stop the narrator from affirming her views. The speech of the narrator is powerful, for it is directed to the actual readers of this book rather than to the imaginary passersby addressed by Lady Zion. We may say that the words of the narrator come closer to representing the "voice of God" or the word of God. But whereas human perpetrators stop at nothing to silence their victims, God in his sovereignty and mercy has allowed these laments to be preserved. He allowed these words recounting his negative actions against his own people to be preserved in what we now call Holy Scriptures!

2:9–13 THE EFFECT OF GOD'S ACTIONS ON ZION

We often speak in terms of directions when we describe our emotional lives, saying that things are "looking up" or that we are "feeling down."[6] As the narrator describes the effects of God's actions on Lady Zion, he uses the same type of language. There is a noticeable "downward" movement in the next section of the chapter:

- Zion's "gates have sunk into the ground" (v. 9)
- "The elders . . . sit on the ground" (v. 10)
- The poet's own "heart is poured on the ground" (v. 11), as he sees "children and infants faint in the streets" (v. 11)

The only upward movement is when the elders sprinkle dust on their heads[7] (v. 10) and the children raise their voice to cry out for food (v. 12).

Earlier, "the ramparts and the walls" were said to lament their destruction (v. 8). Now in verse 9 the focus is on the gates. In ancient Israel, the gates were "the place of commercial, legal, and social activity."[8] It was there that decisions were made and guidance sought. But where are the people to go for justice and good government now? The gates are nowhere to be found. They "have sunk into the ground." The king and the princes have been "exiled

---

6. See Lakoff and Johnson, *Metaphors We Live By*. See also Philip D. King, *Surrounded by Bitterness: Image Schemas and Metaphors for Conceptualizing Distress in Classical Hebrew* (Eugene, OR: Pickwick Publications, 2012).
7. The word "sprinkle" comes from the Hebrew verb *'alah*, which means "to go up."
8. Berlin, *Lamentations*, 71.

among the nations" (v. 9). Therefore "the law is no more" (v. 9). The word translated "law" comes from the Hebrew word *torah,* which in the present context means "instruction." The king and the leaders, as God's representatives, were to uphold the will of the Lord. But they are no longer able to do that because they have vanished from the land.

The last line of verse 9 mentions "the prophets." The fact that they are mentioned last may be an indication of their importance. They were God's spokespersons, declaring what the Lord requires and intends. In a way, their responsibility was even higher than that of the king and other leaders. The latter depended on the prophet for a word from the Lord. But the prophets "no longer find visions from the LORD."

The source of the prophets' message was supposed to be "the LORD" (v. 9). Unfortunately, the prophets deceived the people (see v. 14). The words of the prophet Hosea to the priests had become true even among the prophets: "my people are destroyed from lack of knowledge" (Hos 4:6). The priests Hosea was speaking to had been rejected by Yahweh because they "ignored the law of . . . God" (Hos 4:6). When either priest or prophet speak their own words rather than God's word, the church and the nation are in grave danger.

This is why in verse 10 we find everyone mourning, from the old to the young: The "elders . . . sit on the ground in silence" and the "young women . . . have bowed down their heads to the ground" (Lam 2:10). Their posture recalls that of Lady Zion as she sat alone (1:1).

All these seated figures are in a posture of mourning (see 1:1). But whereas Lady Zion is said to sit alone, the elders sit "in silence."[9] Why are they silent? Probably because "overwhelming suffering is language-destroying. Physical pain is unsharable because it attacks both dignity and identity and so its force destroys speech."[10]

When those who are suffering no longer want to speak, someone else has to speak for them. In verse 11, the narrator steps back and the poet takes charge. I agree with Mintz that here the poet is speaking not as the narrator but as the poet himself.[11] The latter can no longer keep quiet as he sees the suffering of the children. Earlier, the poet spoke as the narrator in a way that

---

9. Some scholars understand the verb *damam* in the sense of "to lament" or "to weep." But as Renkema rightly points out the parallel in 3:26, 28 goes against this view. The verb here has the meaning "to be silent" (Renkema, *Lamentations,* 263–264).

10. O'Connor, *Lamentations and the Tears of the World* (Maryknoll, NY: Orbis, 2002) 101. She cites Elaine Scarry, *The Body in Pain: The Making and Unmaking of the World* (New York: Oxford University Press, 1985), 35.

11. Mintz, "Rhetoric of Lamentations," 6.

was similar to an objective reporter. But his reaction in verse 11 and his words to Daughter Zion in verse 13 betray his inner feelings. He is no objective, distant narrator. Rather, he stands by the side of Lady Zion, identifying with her, weeping with her and especially with her children, who "faint in the streets of the city." In place of the silence of the elders, we hear the voice of the poet as he shares his own pain at the sight of his people's suffering: "My eyes fail from weeping, I am in torment within" (2:11). What finally forces the poet to speak "is not the spectre of state and temple destroyed but a domestic detail from the horrors of the siege: children expiring from hunger in the streets of the city."[12]

The elders are silent, but not the children. They are crying out to their mothers, "Where is bread and wine?" (v. 12). In the OT children are normally silent; we do not hear them speak. But now we do hear them asking their mothers for "bread and wine." There have been some discussions about why they ask specifically for "bread and wine," but such discussions distract us from the main point of the text. Suffice it to say that these words would be a bitter reminder of the good life the people enjoyed before their enemies destroyed everything. Wine was reserved for special people and special occasions (see Gen 14:18). The word translated "bread" (Lam 2:12) is literally "grain" in Hebrew. In the Psalms corn or grain is a symbol of prosperity (e.g. Ps 65:9). So maybe we can say that "bread and wine" reflects how children view their mothers. They expect nothing but the best from them, even in times of disaster. But there is no response from these mothers. They are as helpless as their dying children, whose "lives ebb away in their mothers' arms" (v. 12). A similar image is found in the "Lamentation over the Destruction of Ur," where the poet speaks of "The young lying on their mothers' laps, like fish were carried off by the waters.[13]

Deeply disturbed by the sight of the suffering children, the poet speaks directly to Lady Zion for the first time.[14] Whereas earlier he had attempted to deal with his people's tragedy by portraying Jerusalem and all its inhabitants as a woman mourning her loss, now he extends the metaphor and actually

---

12. Ibid.

13. Kramer, "Lamentation," 455–463.

14. Here we see a more sophisticated use of personification. Earlier, we commented that personification allows us to create some distance between us and our experience, enabling us to deal with our pain and suffering. It also allows us to see our situation from different vantage points. Lanahan defines it as "a creative procedure in the displacement of the poet's imagination beyond the limitations of his single viewpoint so that he may gain a manifold insight into the human experience" (Lanahan, "Speaking Voice," 41).

speaks to her, asking four questions and making one statement. The four questions are all in verse 13:

- What can I say for you?
- With what can I compare you?
- To what can I liken you?
- Who can heal you?

We often come to people who are suffering with answers rather than questions. We are there not to listen but to say something. We assume we already know all the answers. In contrast to this, the poet comes to Lady Zion not with answers, but with questions. His first question was "What can I say for you?" Observe that he is not concerned about saying something *to* Lady Zion but in saying something *for* her. The Hebrew word translated "say" comes from a word that means "bear witness." In our attempt to help those who suffer, we may be too much concerned with what we will say to them. But often the last thing they need is a word of advice. What they need is someone who will "bear witness" for them. As we noted above, extreme pain and trauma can make one unable to speak. Thus it can be important for survivors to have people who will give words to their pain and validate their experience. The narrator did this in the early part of this chapter. Such retelling of the experience is itself an act of compassion for a voiceless sufferer. What the poet has been doing is actually his own way of bearing witness to Zion's suffering. Without offering a sermon or word of encouragement, he has actually offered help.

The next two questions are related; they are to do with the search for something with which the poet can compare Lady Zion's suffering: "With what can I compare you . . . To what can I liken you?" (v. 13). The poet is seeking for a metaphor "that I may comfort you" (v. 13). As we said earlier when talking about metaphors and personification, the ability to give a name to one's experience is an important step towards recovery. When we go through tragic experiences, we tend to feel overwhelmed. There is just so much going on that we lose a handle on things, and on life itself. And so long as we grapple with an unnamed 'thing' we will continue to grope in the dark. But by using a metaphor to "name" it, we gain some control. So the poet tells Lady Zion: "Your wound is as deep as the sea" (v. 13). This is the only utterance in this verse which is not a question but a courageous lament. It honestly confronts the hopelessness of the situation. This hopelessness is reinforced by the last question: "Who can heal you?" (v. 13)

2:14–17 "WHO CAN HEAL YOU?"

The poet answers his own question by listing four possible healers: the prophets (v. 14), the passersby (v. 15), the enemies (v. 16), and the Lord himself (v. 17). Instead of bringing healing, each of the four made Lady Zion's wounds worse.

2:14 The prophets

The prophets represent the spiritual leaders of the people. They could have averted the punishment had they proclaimed the word of the Lord and called on the people to repent. Instead, they gave visions that were "false and worthless" (v. 14). Their failure to receive a vision from God (see v. 9) is an indication of their spiritual blindness.

Failure to hear from God or receive visions from him can be an indication of his judgment. We see this in the story of Eli the priest (1 Sam 2–3). Like the prophets in Lamentations 2:9, Eli no longer received a vision from God nor heard from him. Instead, God had to speak to the boy Samuel. This judgment from God was a result of Eli's failure to implement God's will in his own household by allowing his own children to continue in their evil ways.

Whenever we compromise God's word, we distance ourselves from him until our heart and our ears become so callous we no longer hear him speaking to us. When we seek human praise rather than being committed to doing the will of God, we bring ourselves and our people into grave danger. "The condemnation of the prophets should trouble the church, and particularly its leadership. The church is meant to be a conscience for the nation. Its leaders are called to speak the word of God boldly and with confidence. However, if church leaders become corrupt, the people will also become corrupt and will have no message for the world."[15] Unfortunately, the prophets who were supposed to proclaim the word of the Lord to the people utterly failed in their task. Instead of declaring repentance they preached peace. Eager to hear the clapping and applause of their followers, they led the people to their own destruction.

2:15 The passersby

In Hebrew, the first word of verse 15 is related to the word "clap" (*safaq*). The prophets longed to hear human clapping rather than God's word. The

---

15. Paul Swarup, "Lamentations," in *South Asia Bible Commentary* (India: Open Doors Publications, 2015), 1023.

result is that "all who pass your way clap their hands at you" clapping is not applause but an insult. Those who are looki will find a punch.[16]

The passersby were first mentioned in 1:12 when Lady Zion pou. her heart to them. There was no one else with whom she could share her pain (see 1:12–16).[17] We were not told how they responded to her words. But here in chapter 2 we do hear their response, and it is brutal. Rather than showing sympathy, they scoff at Lady Zion: "Is this the city that was called the perfection of beauty, the joy of the whole earth?" (2:15). They have turned their backs on her in her need. This is one of the sad realities when we pour out our hearts to other people. Sometimes, instead of being a help to us, they gossip about us and turn what we shared with them against us. They become our enemies. That is why we need to be careful with whom we share our laments. We need people like the poet of Lamentations who is willing to listen to us and cares deeply for us.

2:16 The enemies

The actions of the next "potential healer" are predictable. Like the passersby, the enemies insult and even "gnash their teeth" at Lady Zion (v. 16). Verse 16 reiterates what the poet has said earlier: their enemies have become their "head" (see 1:5). They are the ones who can say, "This is the day we have waited for; we have lived to see it" (2:16). The phrase translated "we have lived" is literally "we have found." This is the same verb used in Lamentations 1:3 and 6. While Lady Zion and her princes can find no rest, her enemies have succeeded in everything. What is more, their enemies are able to say, "we have seen" (2:16) whereas Lady Zion keeps calling on God to see her sufferings (1:9, 11). Later in chapter 2 she repeats the same cry (2:20). But God does not seem to see her. Her enemies' declaration, "We have swallowed her up," recalls God's action of swallowing up Israel (vv. 2, 5, 8). God has become like one of her enemies.

2:17 God

God himself is mentioned last in the "list" of potential healers. This is because he is the most important of the possible healers. Everything depends on him. But verse 17 explains why he does not heal and gives us a more complete picture of why the people have suffered so. Not only did their prophets failed

---

16. *Ang naghahanap ng palakpak, ang aabutin ay sapak.*
17. In Filipino, we say, *nagsumbong siya.*

to proclaim God's message to them, God has also "fulfilled his word, which he decreed long ago." God warned the people through Moses that if they refused to obey his commandments, they would suffer under their enemies. Because their spiritual leaders failed in their task of reminding them of what the Lord had said, the people experienced disaster. Rather than being their healer and comforter, God has become like their enemies. Instead of defending them, he has "exalted the horn of your foes." How can you win if God is against you? The poem is consistent. God has purposely turned against his people. The savior has become the enemy.

Where can Lady Zion go? Where can she find the healing she needs? All her leaders, including her spiritual counsellors, have failed. Even God has closed heaven's doors to her and hurled judgments on her. Where can she turn?

2:18–22 "POUR OUT YOUR HEART LIKE WATER IN THE PRESENCE OF THE LORD"

In the light of everything that God has done to Lady Zion, some scholars argue that the time has come for Lady Zion to "talk back" to her Lord. Speaking like divorce lawyers, they counsel Lady Zion to leave her husband, the Lord. Mandolfo[18] quotes Diamond and O'Connor who write:

> The monologue of the injured husband alone is our source of information about this marriage. As often happens in divorce, it may be that the husband exaggerates the crimes of his spouse, blames her for everything wrong in the relationship, and makes as a condition of her return her acceptance of that blame. We hear him interrogate her belligerently and accuse her with his version of her words. . . . What would happen if female Israel told the story? Would she tell of her husband's verbal abuse, his foolish jealousy, his despicable exaggerations?"[19]

But we have seen in Lamentations 1 that Lady Zion never let go of her God (see Lam 1:18–20). She continues to cling to him as her Lord and husband. Likewise, the poet, far from advising Lady Zion to abandon her God, calls on her to draw near to God and cry out to him.

---

18. Mandolfo, *Daughter Zion*, 19.
19. A. R. Pete Diamond and Kathleen M. O'Connor, "Unfaithful Passions: Coding Women Coding Men in Jeremiah 2–3," *Biblical Interpretation* 4 (1996), 309–310.

The opening words of verse 18 literally read, "Their heart cried to the Lord."[20] But this is puzzling as the word "heart" is very rarely used as subject of the verb "cried." Moreover, all the other verbs in verses 18–19 are commands, in the imperative voice. Thus some argue that the opening line of verse 18 should also be a command: "Cry out from the heart to the Lord."[21] But it should be noted that even if we follow the literal reading of the text, the point remains the same. In fact, it even strengthens our argument, for even before the narrator exhorts Lady Zion to pour out her heart to God, the people have already been doing it.

The narrator admonishes Lady Zion to "let your tears flow like a river day and night" (v. 18b). She has been weeping bitterly, her tears flowing down her cheeks (1:2). The narrator urges her to shed more tears, this time without any attempt to stop their flow (v. 18c).

"Arise, cry out in the night"

Strange as it may seem, continuous crying and weeping before the Lord are a sign of hope.[22] The opposite is also true. It is those who are in despair who say, "I have no more tears to shed." The narrator is calling on Zion to cry out to the Lord because he still believes God is present, and that though God has acted "without pity," he can once more show mercy and compassion. That is why he urges her to "arise" (v. 19). Thus far, the dominant movement has been downward (see above) but here for the first time in the whole of chapter 2 there is a movement upwards with a positive connotation. In addition to the call to "arise," Lady Zion is to "lift up" her hands to the Lord. She is to "cry out in the night" (v. 19).

2:19 "Pour out your heart like water in the presence of the Lord"

Crying is to be understood in relation to prayer: "pour out your heart like water in the presence of the Lord" (v. 19). "Pouring out one's heart like water" means opening up one's heart to God, being honest to him about what one truly feels. This is communication of the most intimate kind, what we in

---

20. This is the reading reflected in the MT and LXX.

21. After surveying various possibilities, Salters, *Lamentations*, 168–169, opted for reading the first word as an imperative feminine singular directed to Daughter Zion: "Cry out." The second word is then understood adverbially as "from the heart."

22. See the article by Yohanna Katanacho, "Cry with Us." Online at http://www.bmsworldmission.org/news- blogs/archive/a-poem-lament-both-sides-gaza (accessed on December 1, 2014).

the Philippines call *loob sa loob* (literally, "inner to inner" or "heart to heart"). There are only a few people with whom we can share our hearts like this, for it takes time and nurturing for this kind of relationship to be established. This is true both of our relationship with other people and with God. Only those who practice being open to God about everything will learn what it means to be honest with God even when it hurts.

In Lamentations 2:19 the pouring out of one's heart is done "in the presence of the Lord." This is characteristic of biblical lament. It means that all experience, including negative experiences, have a place in his presence. Prayer is not just the nice and orderly words we utter to God. Even if the words are without order, these become whole in his presence.[23] We do not have to hide our pain or questions from him. It is okay to admit these before the Lord. We can pour our hearts in the context of our relationship with God and in a spirit of reverence.

It is true that not all questioning and lamenting are acceptable to God. We know this from the desert experience of the Israelites. God was not pleased when they kept on complaining, with the result that many of them were destroyed. But the lament that is acceptable to God flows from an honest heart that longs to be restored to God. Lady Zion may hurl her laments at God (see vv. 20–22 below), but she never let go of God.

There is a lot of lamenting in the world today. Many people weep and cry, complain and lament, but not before God. Many just weep, with no one to listen to them. For others, pouring out one's heart is not an easy thing to do. This may be because of their cultural background, or for theological reasons, or because they have had negative experiences in the past. Lady Zion had such experiences when she shared her heart with the passersby (1:12–16), only to be rejected and insulted by them (2:15). But the words of the poet to Lady Zion indicate his view of God. The difference between lamenting to people and before God is that with the former we may be rejected. That is why we need to be careful about whom we expressing our heart to. But with God, we can be assured that our honest laments will be accepted. "Wherever one looks in the Bible, the sincere words of a sufferer, however incriminating, are acceptable in God's sight."[24]

Verse 19 ends with another upward movement – "Lift up your hands to him for the lives of your children" (v. 19c). Here we see the centrality of the

---

23. *Kahit tagpi-tagpi ang mga salita, nabubuo pagdating sa kanyang presensiya.* Hobbins, "Zion's Plea," 173.
24. Ibid.

children. It was the suffering of the children that brought tears to the poet's eyes (v. 11). Verse 19 is the longest verse in this chapter, and its description of the children "who faint from hunger at every street corner" (v. 19d) captures its emphasis.

2:20-22 Lady Zion pours out her heart to the Lord

In verses 20–22 Lady Zion does what the poet has asked her to do. Here we have an example of an actual pouring out of one's heart to the Lord, which involves being honest about one's feelings about what God has done. Lady Zion cries out to the Lord: "Look, LORD, and consider: Whom have you ever treated like this?" (v. 20a). The first four words are exactly the same as her earlier address to God in Lamentations 1:11.

Her question in verse 20 looks back to the previous verse, with a play on the Hebrew word *alal*, "you treated," and *'olal*, the word translated "children" in verse 19: "Should women eat their offspring, the children (*'olal*) they have cared for?" (v. 20b). This is the worst possible scenario in anyone's experience – cannibalism committed by the mothers themselves. It will be mentioned again in 4:10.

Lady Zion's question is an expression of anger. She is angry at God and she does not hide it. Instead, she pours out her anger to God. In the first part of this chapter, we heard a lot about God's anger. But now it is Lady Zion's turn to be angry. She cannot understand how God can allow little children to suffer.

In the last line of verse 20, Lady Zion asks another question: "Should priest and prophet be killed in the sanctuary of the Lord?" Priests and prophets were among the main representatives of the Lord to the people. They were supposed to be closest to God. Moreover, there was a belief that if you hid in the sanctuary, God would protect you. But God's closest servants have died in the very place where God's presence ought to be present. This brings us back to verse 1, which spoke of God's footstool. Now we understand why the narrator said that God "has not remembered his footstool." If there was no protection even for the priest and prophet, how much hope was there for the rest of the people?

It thus comes as no surprise that "young and old lie together in the dust of the streets" (v. 21a). The phrase "young and old" is a literary device that means "everyone." In the next line, Lady Zion becomes more specific as she speaks of "my young women and my young men" (ESV) who have fallen by the sword. The NIV reverses the order, and mentions the young men first.

But that is not the order in the Hebrew text. The women may well have been deliberately mentioned first to bring home the cruelty of it all. In a battle, it is the young men, the soldiers, who die first; here it is the young women who die. The most painful of all is that this is something God himself has done: "You have slain them . . . you have slaughtered them without pity" (v. 21c). This is the third time the words, "without pity" have been used in this chapter. In the first two instances, the narrator was describing God's actions (vv. 2, 17). But here Lady Zion tells God directly, "you have slaughtered them without pity" (v. 21c). And this was something that God did deliberately: "you summoned against me terrors on every side" (v. 22).

The chapter ends with Lady Zion turning her gaze away from the Lord and addressing her audience: "In the day of the LORD's anger no one escaped or survived; those I cared for and reared my enemy has destroyed" (v. 22). Who is this enemy – the Lord or the Babylonians? God has been described as "like an enemy" (vv. 3-5), but there is still a distinction between God and the human enemy. The fact that Lady Zion continues to come to God suggests that here the "enemy" is not God but the Babylonians.[25]

But one notices a distancing, a drawing away of Lady Zion from God. She becomes like the narrator who reports what God has done instead of talking to God directly about it. This reminds us that pouring out one's heart to God does not mean everything will be alright once again. Restoration is a process that involves the painful journey of honest pouring out of one's heart.

---

25. Brady, *Rabbinic Targum*, 35, warns us to be careful not to read too many of our modern concepts into the ancient text. Lady Zion does not go so far as to call God "my enemy."

LAMENTATIONS 3

One of the problems we face when confronted with tragic experiences is that we tend to have only one explanation – the tragedy has occurred because we have done something wrong; God is punishing us. This is the most common view in the Bible as well as in traditional Asian contexts. Thus during Typhoon Yolanda the most common prayer uttered by our people was "Forgive us, Lord." Many such prayers were written on pieces of paper and posted on the ship found in one of the villages.

But we know that tragic experiences are complex. Limiting ourselves to one explanation makes us insensitive to the complexities of other people's experience.[1] How can we tell a little girl who has lost her entire family that it is because of her sin that this has happened? How do we cope with ongoing suffering? What do we say to people who remain in a desperate situation even after they have repented of their sins and have done everything they can to survive? How do we live our faith in the midst of the continuing realities of pain and suffering?

The good thing about Lamentations 3 is that it is not limited to one perspective. Opposing views are aired with no attempt to resolve them. This may be disconcerting to those who wish for one clear answer. But our poet is wise. He himself has gone through affliction (v. 1). Like Lady Zion he has tasted the wrath of God (vv. 1–16). Yet precisely at the lowest point of his experience, when he had lost all hope, he found his song in the night. Declaring that "the steadfast love of the LORD never ceases" (v. 22, ESV), he exhorts those who suffer to put their trust in God (v. 25). They are to bear their suffering in submission to God (vv. 26–30). God is merciful and will not allow his people to suffer forever (vv. 31–33). Instead of complaining (v. 39), they should repent and turn back to God (vv. 40–42a).

The speaker in Lamentations 3 endorses the traditional response to suffering that recommends submission and repentance. But he is not limited by this point of view. He also sees the need to pour out one's heart to God. Repentance does not invalidate lament. Submission does not mean questions are no longer allowed. Thus, even after offering a confession to God (v. 42a), the man utters a complaint to God: "you have not forgiven" (v. 42b). What follows is a communal lament (vv. 43–66) interspersed with words uttered

---

1. See Bernard Adeney-Risakotta, "Is There a Meaning in Natural Disasters? Constructions of Culture, Religion, and Science," *Exchange* 38 (2009): 226–243.

by the man himself (vv. 48–63). Reading these verses in parallel to the preceding section (vv. 25–42), it becomes clear that there is no one voice in Lamentations 3. In fact, there are contradictory voices. Yet it is encouraging that all these voices are heard. No voice is suppressed.

3:1–16 "I AM THE MAN WHO HAS SEEN AFFLICTION"

Lamentations 3 is unique. Unlike the previous chapters, it does not begin with *eikha* (compare 1:1; 2:1) and we do not hear the voice of Lady Zion. In chapter 3, the voice we hear is that of the "man who has seen affliction" (v. 1).

Who is this man? There has been a lot of discussion about his identity. Some argue that he is Jeremiah. However, there is no way we can be sure who he is. We also have to bear in mind that in Lamentations we are dealing with poetry.[2] Just as he created the personification of Lady Zion, so the author could have created a "man" who represents "Everyman."[3]

Although I agree with this view, we should also not lose sight of the uniqueness of this man. He is not just "Everyman"; he is one "who has seen affliction by the rod of his wrath" (v. 1, ESV).[4] Not everyone can say that. This man is like Lady Zion in that he knows what it means to experience God's anger. He himself has "seen" it. This gives him authority to speak about the proper response to God in the face of suffering. He can bear testimony to his own experience of God's wrath and to how, despite this, he has regained hope. He is therefore someone who has the "right" to speak to Lady Zion and others who have gone through extreme suffering. His words are in part a response to the painful ending of chapter 2, which accused God of violence. However, this should not be seen as the sole function of chapter 3.

The man's testimony to having experienced God's wrath links this chapter to the previous ones. In chapter 1, Lady Zion shared the pain she experienced as a result of the pouring out of God's wrath upon her (1:12–16). In chapter 2, the narrator identified with Lady Zion and spoke of how God had expressed his anger (2:1–8). Here the man testifies that he has gone through a

---

2. Mintz writes: "Proposing historical identities for the speaker is the kind of speculation which is not only destined to indeterminacy but is also of doubtful relevance to a literary analysis. . . . Attempts to find a single, consistent solution throughout the chapter [chap 3] are condemned to be defeated, not by the poem's lack of unity, but by its complexity" (Mintz, "Rhetoric of Lamentations," 9).
3. For the view that the man represents "Everyman," see Hillers, *Lamentations*, 122.
4. The NIV speaks of "the LORD's wrath," but in the Hebrew the phrase is merely "his wrath." But the pronoun "his" clearly refers to God.

similar experience to Lady Zion. There is thus a progression in these chapters, from describing suffering, to identifying with it, to sharing in it as one who has had the same experience.

Verse 2 begins with the word "me" in Hebrew, as if the poet is trying to say, "Yes, it happened to me; I myself have experienced this." It is "me" whom God has "driven away," and has made to walk in "darkness rather than light" (v. 2). These words stand in dramatic contrast to the beloved Psalm 23. There the Lord uses his rod to guide his sheep into green pastures. In Lamentations 3, the rod is used to drive the man into a place of darkness. Instead of being led by God, the man is driven away from him.[5]

To further emphasize his experience of the wrath of God, the man says, "indeed, he has turned his hand against me" (v. 3). What's more, his experience is not a one-time thing but a repeated one: "again and again, all day long" (v. 3). His suffering is like that of Job. God allowed Job to lose his possessions. Later, his children were killed. Then he lost his health when God responded to the adversary's words: "Skin for skin! A man will give all he has for his own life. But now stretch out your hand and strike his flesh and bones, and he will surely curse you to your face" (Job 2:4–5). The man in Lamentations 3 uses the same words from the passage in Job ("skin," "flesh," and "bone") to describe what God has done to him: "He has made my flesh and my skin waste away; he has broken my bones" (Lam 3:4). Like Job, he is surrounded by "bitterness and hardship" (v. 5; see also v. 15). This man can hear the words of Job's wife: "Curse God and die!" (Job 2:9). Though he is still alive, bitterness and darkness fill his life: "He has made me dwell in darkness like those long dead" (Lam 3:6).

In verses 7–9, the man speaks of himself not merely as a sufferer but as being like a prisoner, confined so that he cannot escape (v. 7). Even if he cries for help, no one will answer him. His prayers are shut out (v. 8). Everywhere he turns, there are obstacles (v. 9). There is no way out. Even if he did somehow manage to escape, God would be like a "bear lying in wait, like a lion in hiding" (v. 10). Centuries earlier, David had talked about how he had protected his sheep from lions and bears when he was a shepherd boy (1 Sam 17:34) and later he testified how God has been a shepherd to him (Ps 23). But that is not this man's experience. To him, God is more like a bear who "dragged me from the path and mangled me" (Lam 3:11). God has made this man his

---

5. The Hebrew word used in Lam 3:2 is *nahag*, whereas in Ps 23:3 it is *nakha*. But the two words are similar in sound, and the former is also used in the positive sense of leading (see Ps 78:52).

target (v. 12), the object at which he aimed his arrows, piercing his heart (v. 13). Not only has God broken his heart, he has also broken "my teeth with gravel" (v. 16). This is what the psalmist asked the Lord to do in Psalm 3:7: "break the teeth of the wicked." Thus the opening section of Lamentations 3 is full of words that imply violence, words that vividly remind us of the complaint in Lamentations 2:2 that the Lord is "without pity."

Looking beyond the poetic language, can we tell what specific experience the man is talking about? We note that there is an abundance of military imagery in the references to being a prisoner, a target, arrows, etc. It will become clear towards the end of this chapter that the man is referring to his enemies and what they did to him (vv. 64–66). All those who had suffered at the hands of the Babylonians would be able to relate to his experience. In verse 14 the man speaks of having become a "laughingstock." This is the state of the nation. Their defeat and subsequent exile have led to their being taunted by their enemies.

It thus appears that all the violence is done by the Babylonians and is not the result of God's direct action. But since the speaker and the people believe that God allowed the Babylonians to do these things, the man can speak of the destruction as God's own doing.

3:17–24 HOPE IN THE MIDST OF HOPELESSNESS

The bitterness, darkness, and all the violence he has experienced have taken their toll on the man. He feels "deprived of peace" (v. 17). In Filipino we have a saying, "*habang may buhay, may pag-asa*" [While there's life, there's hope]. But the man in Lamentations 3 has nothing to look forward to: "all that I had hoped from the LORD" is "gone" (v. 18).

Yet it is at his lowest point, precisely where he thinks he has lost all hope, that the man first refers to the Lord, using his covenant name "Yahweh." This is the first time the name of the Lord occurs in Lamentations 3. In all the previous verses, the man referred to God using only the third person pronoun "he."

I remember my own experience when as a young boy I lay shivering because of a very high fever, afraid that I was about to die. Everyone else was asleep, and I did not want to waken them. I desperately tried to keep myself warm, but was failing and about to faint. Then I uttered the name "Jesus," which I had learned from my mother who taught me in Sunday School. I don't know how it happened, but suddenly I was able to sleep like a baby. The following day, I was able to get up, well and strong.

In uttering the name of the Lord, the man remembered there is hope in the Lord. It is not that the name is some kind of magic formula. Rather, the name Yahweh reminds him of the covenant relationship between God and his people (see Exod 3:12–15) and of how God reached down to his people in the midst of their suffering. The people have come to know that no one who hopes in the Lord will be abandoned (Ps 9:10). The man in Lamentations 3 has learned that his endurance may falter, but God's steadfast love never ceases (see v. 22).

The amazing thing is that even though God is viewed as the one who caused his sufferings (vv. 1–16), God is still the one to whom the man appeals to for help. Like Lady Zion, he cries out to the Lord: "Remember my affliction and my wanderings, the wormwood and the gall!" (v. 19, ESV; compare 1:9, 11). The NIV translates this as "I remember," so that the man is the one doing the remembering. It may have made this change because the sudden cry to God appears to interrupt the flow of the poem.[6] But we have seen exclamations like this before in the book of Lamentations. In chapters 1 and 2 Lady Zion interrupted the narrator by crying out to the Lord for help: "O LORD, behold my affliction" (1:9; 2:20). Here in 3:19, the man does not begin his cry with "O LORD" because he has just mentioned the name of the Lord in the previous verse (and also possibly because he needs space in the line to make room for his petition[7]).

The man used four words to describe his situation: affliction, wandering, bitterness, and gall (v. 19). The first word occurred at the beginning of the chapter where the speaker identified himself as the "man who has seen affliction" (v. 1). "Wandering" may refer to homelessness, either through exile or as a way of describing all their experience (see 1:3). The last two words refer to wormwood (see ESV) and gall, two substances that are particularly bitter in taste and so make good metaphors for bitterness.

The man asks the Lord to "remember" all of his sufferings. As used here, the word "remember" does not mean mere intellectual knowledge, as if he is

---

6. The NIV translation of v. 19 follows the LXX. But the MT has the imperative form of the verb, as reflected in the ESV. I prefer the reading reflected in the ESV which takes the verb as a petition: "Remember my affliction" (3:19, ESV).

7. If so, this is an example of ellipsis. The acrostic structure of this chapter may also be at work here. The word "remember" (zekhar) fits in with the Hebrew acrostic in v. 19, whereas the name of the Lord, Yahweh, would not.

assuming that God has stopped thinking about him. Rather, it has the sense of doing something, as God did when he "remembered Noah" (Gen 8:1). God's remembering is equivalent to his action (see also Gen 19:29).

God is asked to "remember" the man's suffering because the man's own memories leave him "downcast" (Lam 3:20). The more he remembers his experience, the more bereft of peace and happiness he becomes. But when he calls "this" to mind he begins to have hope (v. 21). The word "this" forms the first word of verse 21 in Hebrew and points forward to an affirmation: "The steadfast love of the LORD never ceases; his mercies never come to an end; they are new every morning; great is your faithfulness" (vv. 22–23, ESV).[8]

Verses 22 and 23 have been included in hymns and popular worship songs. They are probably the only verses in the book of Lamentations that many people know.[9] Unfortunately, however, they are often quoted or sung without regard to their context, which means that we fail to properly appreciate their significance.

Verse 22 speaks about God's "steadfast love." These two words are a translation of one Hebrew word, *hesed*, which refers to God's commitment of love to his people. Though everything else will fail, God's faithfulness remains. The other word related to "steadfast love" is "mercies" or "compassions" (*rakhamim*). When elderly people say *"May awa ang Diyos"* [God is merciful] when they are in a difficult situation, they are using the word in the way in which it is used in Lamentations 3. The man had been recounting his experience of affliction and of the wrath of God (vv. 1, 19). (Although the word "wrath" occurs only in v. 1, the whole of vv. 12–16 pertains to his experience of God's wrath.) Thus, we are surprised when the man suddenly starts

---

8. NIV follows the MT reading for the verb *tamam* in v. 22, translating it with the first person plural suffix: "we are not consumed." But the verb with the first person plural pronominal suffix (*tamnu*) can be obtrusive in a section which mainly employs the first person singular. This has led some to follow the reading found in the Syriac and Targum (see BHS notes) which has a third person plural verb (*tammu*) (see Bertil Albrektson, *Studies in the Text and Theology of Lamentations*, Vol. 21, Studia Theologica Lundensia [Lund: Gleerup, 1963], 145). I follow the MT in the above translation. Compare the translation of Albrektson, 145: "It is Yhwh's mercies that we are not consumed, his compassions fail not."

9. It is unfortunate that vv. 22–24 are missing in the LXX. If this reflected the original manuscript, their absence would be significant for these verses are the only hymnic affirmation of Yahweh's attributes in the passage. But the absence of the verses in the LXX is probably a case of a homoioteleuton. In other words, the translator's eye skipped a few lines because of the similarity in the endings of vv. 21b (*'al ken okil*) and 24b (*'al ken okil lo*). The context of v. 21 anticipates the positive affirmations in vv. 22–24 and the presence of v. 21 in the MT is a strong testimony to the authenticity of the Hebrew text (see Iain W. Provan, *Lamentations* [Grand Rapids, MI: Eerdmans], 93).

speaking of God's steadfast love and mercy. How can he talk about God's love and mercy after all he has experienced of God's wrath? But it is precisely in extreme suffering that we see the reality of God's mercy. When we are in utter darkness, we notice even the smallest glimmer of light.

The man proclaims that "the LORD is my portion" (v. 24). Elsewhere in the Old Testament, the word "portion" is used of the portion of the land of Israel that was given as an inheritance to each of the tribes of Israel, except the Levites. To say, God is my "portion" means he is the only one on whom we depend. As the psalmist declares: "Whom have I in heaven but you? And earth has nothing I desire besides you" (Ps 73:25).

With verses 22–24 we are in the "heart" of the book of Lamentations. It is the peak of the mountain as it were. One would wish never to leave it, like Peter who asked Jesus if they could remain on the Mount of Transfiguration. But like the disciples, we all need to go down from the mountain. The journey continues. In the following sections, the man again confronts the reality of life.

3:25–42 WORDS OF ADVICE FROM THE "MAN"

After speaking in the first person ("I") the man turns to his audience to give advice to those who are going through similar experiences.[10] At the beginning of the chapter he refers to himself as "the man" (*geber*) (v. 1). Here he addresses the "man" (*geber*). This noun appears three times in this section (vv. 27, 35, and 39). Though his words are addressed to a wider audience, his focus is on the person (whether man or woman) who like him has "seen affliction" under the Lord's wrath (v. 1).[11] His own experience puts him in a position of authority. He has the right to speak to one who is suffering and give words of advice.

3:25–30 What should those who are suffering do?

Verses 25 to 27 all begin with the word "good" (*tob*) in Hebrew, though this is not reflected in the English translation:

- "The LORD is *good* to those whose hope is in him" (v. 25)
- "It is *good* to wait quietly" (v. 26)
- "It is *good* for a man to bear the yoke while he is young" (v. 27)

---

10. The same movement is seen in some of the lament psalms. For example, in Psalm 62, the psalmist turns to his audience and exhorts them to pour out their hearts to the Lord (v. 8) after he has related how he lamented and found rest in the Lord (vv. 1-5).

11. Except for the plural in "those whose hope is in him" (v. 25) and "all the prisoners" (v. 34), the rest of the verses are addressed to an individual (see vv. 27–30).

The advice of the man is that those who are suffering should "wait quietly" (v. 26). That is the "good" thing to do. The one who suffers should "sit alone in silence (*damam* in Hebrew)" (v. 28). This is not how Lady Zion responded to suffering. She sits alone (1:1), but she is not quiet; she is weeping (1:2). She cries out to God for help a number of times (1:9, 11, 20–22). The narrator in Lamentations 2 also goes against the man's advice as he commands Lady Zion to "cry out in the night" without ceasing (2:18).

But for the man in Lamentations 3, the proper response to affliction is quiet submission. We are to accept whatever is our lot. As the famous hymn declares, "It is well with my soul." The sufferer is "to bear the yoke laid on him" (v. 27). He is to "bury his face in the dust" (v. 29a). This is a posture of submission. What is striking is that the man admits that his hope is not one hundred percent sure – "there may yet be hope" (v. 29b). Yet despite the absence of certainty, the suffering person ought to continue to submit to the Lord. Even when other people hurl insults at him, presumably because the Lord is not responding to his petitions, he is to accept these insults as part of his lot (v. 30).

3:31–39 Why should the afflicted respond in this way?

Verses 31–39 answer the question of why the afflicted should respond with submission. It is because there is an end to one's suffering. God will not "cast off" forever (v. 31). Alluding to the hymnic words of verses 22–23, the man highlights God's "compassion" (*raham*) and "the abundance of his steadfast love" (v. 32, ESV).[12] God does indeed afflict, but it is not something he willingly does: "he does not afflict from his heart" (v. 33, ESV). This is the opposite of what was said in Lamentations 2:2, where the narrator accused God of acting "without pity."

Verses 34–36 form one long sentence. Each verse begins with an infinitive – "to crush" (v. 34), "to deny" (v. 35), and "to deprive" (v. 36) and the main verb, "see," is at the end of the sentence (v. 36b). Translated literally, the sentence would read something like this: "To crush underfoot all prisoners in the land, to deny people their rights . . . to deprive them of justice, the Lord does not see." But this presents a problem to translators. Is the man saying that the Lord does not see such things? So the NIV and some other versions transform the main clause into a question: "would not the Lord see such

---

12. The repetition of "steadfast love" and "compassion" or "mercy" indicate that this is the same speaker as in the previous section (cf. v. 22). It also supports the authenticity of verses 22–24.

things?" (v. 36b). Since the following verses are in the form of question, this decision is not unreasonable.[13]

But we need to remember the central importance of "seeing" in Lamentations. Lady Zion has been crying out to the Lord for him to "see" her (1:9, 11; 2:20). In spite of her pleading, God has remained silent. So if the man is saying, "the Lord does not see," he is simply confirming Lady Zion's experience. Like the man, Lady Zion has "seen" affliction but "the Lord does not see." So it is quite possible that what we have here represents a view that challenges the advice given in the preceding verses.[14]

The words of verses 37–39 are Job-like and can be read as a response to the previous verses. To say that "the Lord does not see" is like saying that the Lord is incapable of saving or doing good for his people, or worse that he intends only to do them harm. In response to this, the man argues that nothing happens unless it has been ordained by God: "Who can speak and have it happen if the Lord has not decreed it?" (v. 37). The next verse is similar to Job's response to his wife after the latter told him to give up his faith and curse God: "Is it not from the mouth of the Most High that both calamities (ra'ah) and good things (tob) come?" (v. 38; compare Job 2:10: "Shall we accept good [tob] from God, and not trouble [ra'ah]?"). So there should be no room for complaining: "Why should the living complain when punished for their sins?" (Lam 3:39). This verse reflects the general view that the calamity is caused by their sin.

In view of the people's sins, the man calls on everyone to "examine our ways . . . and let us return to the LORD" (v. 40). Note that the man includes himself in the call for heart-searching. Rather than raising our fists against God and questioning his ways, we are to "lift up our hearts and our hands to God in heaven" (v. 41). These words are followed by an actual confession of sins: "We have sinned and rebelled" (v. 42a).

It would have been perfectly understandable had the chapter continued with confession. Yet just like Job, who lamented even after telling his wife to accept everything, including troubles, as coming from God (see, for example, Job 3 where Job cursed the day of his birth), we have a sudden change from

---

13. But see ESV, which translates v. 36b as a statement, though it does not translate the verb as "see" but as "approve."
14. For further discussions, see Villanueva, The "Uncertainty of a Hearing," 230–233. See also Delbert R. Hillers, Lamentations, 122.

confession to lament in v. 42b: "you have not forgiven."[15] In the Hebrew the two statements in verse 42 are simply juxtaposed, without even an "and" between them: "We have sinned and rebelled / you have not forgiven."[16] They stand without any explanation, the tension preserved.

3:43–47 Communal lament

Lamentations 3 contains what scholars refer to as a "sudden change of mood."[17] We have seen the man turn from recounting his experience of affliction (vv. 1–21) to proclaiming the "steadfast love of the Lord" (vv. 22–24). This is similar to the famous turn in the Psalms from lament to praise (see Pss 3, 13, 28). But the "change of mood" is not always from lament to praise. As Lamentations 3 demonstrates, it can also move from praise (vv. 22–24) to lament (vv. 43–66). We see a similar movement in Psalms 9/10, 27, and 89.[18]

Unfortunately, many scholars ignore the movement from praise to lament,[19] and that may be why some scholars think that we have a different speaker in the remaining verses of Lamentations 3. They argue that it is unlikely that someone would move on to lament after having uttered praise and given advice about submitting to God and not complaining. But as mentioned above, the reverse movement is not unique to Lamentations 3.[20]

Moreover, this pattern fits with the practice in traditional Filipino-Asian cultures, where an individual may speak on behalf of the community. Prior to this point, "the man" has been speaking for himself; now he speaks for others too, as we can see from the change in the pronoun from first person singular (I/me) to the first person plural (we/us). So it is not impossible that the "man" who spoke in the preceding sections is also the speaker in the rest of the chapter. Certainly, the acrostic structure continues, with no indication of any break that might serve to introduce a new speaker.

---

15. The earlier confessions also show the same movement from confession to lament (see 1:9, 18).

16. See the MT, though the LXX has "and" (*kai*).

17. Joachim Begrich, "Das Priesterliche Heilsorakel," *ZAW* 52, no. 1 (1934): 81–92.

18. Psalms 9 and 10 are actually one psalm as reflected in the use of the Hebrew alphabet to form the psalm. This is reflected in the the LXX which count these as one psalm. The first part (Ps 9) is thanksgiving while the second part (Ps 10) is a lament. Psalm 27 likewise begins with thanksgiving (vv. 1–6) and moves to lament (vv. 7–14). Psalm 89 does the same with vv. 1–37 (thanksgiving) and vv. 38–51 (lament).

19. See Villanueva, *Uncertainty of a Hearing*.

20. Dobbs-Allsopp, *Lamentations*, 124, points out that the shift from thanksgiving to lament expressed in the words "but now you" in Psalm 89:38 is "analogous to the 'but you' in [Lam] 3:42."

Whoever the speaker is, in verses 43–47 we hear a community pouring out their lament to God in the same way that Lady Zion did earlier (see 2:20–22). The opening words of their lament bring us back to where we started in chapter 3: "You have covered yourself with anger and pursued us; you have slain without pity" (v. 43). The word "anger" (*af*) is the same word translated "wrath" in verse 1. It seems that the people are more able to identify with the man's experience of affliction than with his turn to a more positive stance.[21] Despite his advice and words of encouragement, they still pour out their laments. Their accusation that God has acted "without pity" (v. 43; see also 2:2, 21) contradicts the man's words in Lamentations 3:33: "he does not willingly bring affliction or grief to anyone." Just as the man earlier complained that the Lord "shuts out my prayer" (v. 8), so the people protest, "you have wrapped yourself with a cloud so that no prayer can pass through" (v. 44). Instead of quietly accepting their situation, they complain that God has "made us scum and refuse among the nations" (v. 45), as they continue to be despised by their enemies (v. 46).

How are we to understand the contradictions in the chapter? What do these teach us in terms of how we respond to tragic experiences?

In reading Lamentations 3 we have to bear in mind the situation of the people. The contradictions are part of the people's continuing experience of "ruin and destruction" (v. 47). Years after the destruction of Jerusalem, the city has not been rebuilt. The people remain "squatters." According to Weinberg, even forty years later there were still no sign of reconstruction:

> Excavations by Kathleen Kenyon yield a picture of ruin and desolation that confronted the first returnees of 539/8. While some people had no doubt continued to live in Jerusalem, the archaeological picture is one of their squatting among the rubble, which increased as the terrace walls . . . collapsed through lack of care and the debris accumulated in impassable piles on the lower slopes. No great change in the condition of the city occurred until the time of Nehemiah's arrival in 445.[22]

---

21. The same point can be made as regards the superscriptions in the book of Psalms. Thirteen of these contain brief historical notes about the life of David, almost all of which relate to times of trouble such as his adultery or the rebellion of his son Absalom. Why this focus on negative experiences? One explanation is that people find it easier to identify with struggles than with success.

22. S. S. Weinberg, "Post-Exilic Palestine: An Archaeological Report," *Proceedings of the Israel Academy of Sciences and Humanities* 4 (1971), 80; quoted in Daniel Smith-Christopher, "Reassessing the Historical and Sociological Impact of the Babylonian Exile," in *Exile: Old*

In such circumstances, people have to go beyond the "limits" of traditional wisdom. Here the theologies that gave rise to the book of Job and the lament psalms, especially those that move from praise to lament, become indispensable. The beauty of Lamentations 3 lies in its capacity to hold tensions together. It does not silence contradictory voices but allows them to be heard. There is room for tragic experience in the presence of God. There is a place for our honest questioning, despite attempts to contain or control it. Those who are able to continue in silent submission to God despite their suffering have a place in God's presence. But as Clines contends:

> Let Job the patient sufferer be your model, so long as that is possible for you. But when you cannot bear that any longer, let your grief and anger and impatience direct you towards God, for he is ultimately the origin of the suffering, and it is only through encounter with him that the anguish can be relieved.[23]

3:48–66 THE LAMENT OF THE MAN/POET

In verse 48 there is another shift from "we" to "I," from communal lament to individual lament. While it is possible that it is the community who is speaking through the individual, or that the individual is speaking on behalf of the community, it is more likely that from verse 48 onwards we have the poet himself speaking as the "man." This conclusion is supported by the similarity between Lamentations 3:48 and 2:11. Both passages emphasize weeping. No longer able to contain himself as he sees the suffering of Lady Zion, the poet cried out, "My eyes fail from weeping" (2:11). Similarly, the speaker in 3:48 declares, "streams of tears flow from my eyes." His continuing weeping in 3:49 – "my eyes will flow unceasingly, without relief (*hapugah*)" – is similar to the advice given by the poet to Lady Zion – "let your tears flow like river . . . Give yourself no relief (*pugah*)" (2:18).

The man who spoke at the beginning of the chapter with such authority and force is here shown in tears. The Hebrew word *geber* (man) means "strong man" or "hero." But here the hero breaks into tears. Weeping is not just for women!

Testament, Jewish, and Christian Conceptions (New York: Brill, 1997), 16–17.

23. David J. A. Clines, "Job," in *New Bible Commentary*, ed. D. A. Carson, R. T. France, and G. J. Wenham (Leicester: IVP, 1994), 460.

Why is the man crying? The same exact phrase occurs in both passages: "because my people are destroyed" (3:48; compare 2:11). The two speakers are one in their continuing search for an answer from God despite the situation. Earlier, the poet urged Lady Zion to cry out to the Lord and "give yourself no relief" (2:18). Here, the poet himself cries out: "My eyes will flow unceasingly, without relief, until the Lord looks down from heaven and sees" (3:49–50).

Verse 50 reminds us that the central concern in Lamentations is the restoration of the people's relationship with God. Contrary to what some scholars suggest, Lady Zion is not turning her back on her God.[24] "Zion will be consoled if and only if her chosen partner-in-dialogue, the one she simply and nakedly calls *my Lord* and *YHWH*, sees her as she sees herself. If YHWH saw her as she sees herself – even better."[25]

This is something modern readers may find hard to understand. How can one attribute violent acts on God and continue to pursue him?[26] But there are present-day contemporaries of Lady Zion and the man who speaks in Lamentations 3. After Typhoon Yolanda destroyed Tacloban, a photograph was taken of a woman standing in front of a destroyed church, praying. Like most Filipinos, this woman believed that the typhoon was the work of God, and yet she continued to cling on to God. One reason for this is that she has no one else and nowhere else to go. God may be the "punisher," but he is also the only savior.

Similarly, the people may complain to God; they may accuse him of hindering their prayers so that they never reach him. But they will not stop coming to him. In the end, they do not have anyone else to whom they can go to. From their perspective, there is no one else who can bring them out of the pit into which they have fallen. Only the Lord can deliver them. Though they may feel at times that God is "without pity" (v. 43), they want to believe that he is also merciful (see vv. 32–33). The communal lament does not rule out the view expressed in the earlier words of advice.

Thus, the people come to God to tell him of their troubles, or what we call, *pagsusumbong sa Diyos* (literally, "reporting to God"). There is no exact

---

24. As Hobbins, "Zion's Plea," 161, argues against the position of Mandolfo: "In place of Zion of Lam 1:18 who puts her God in the right and herself in the wrong, Mandolfo offers a Zion who puts herself in the right and her God in the wrong."
25. Ibid.
26. The question of whether the punishment goes beyond what the people deserve is a "product of our modern era" (Brady, *Rabbinic Targum*, 3).

equivalent in English. We do not make *sumbong* (report) to just anyone. We come to a person of authority whom we regard as close to us. We come as a person with no power to someone who has power, just as a child would run to his or her father to report a wrong done to him or her.

Verses 52–66 may be read as the people's pouring out of their heart to God. Employing the language of an individual lament, the poet tries to describe the condition of the people before God. His experience is analogous to that of the people. He reports that his enemies "hunted me like a bird" (v. 52). He finds himself "in a pit" (v. 53), with his enemies throwing stones at him. As before, everything he had hoped for is gone (v. 18). The individual is "about to perish" (v. 54).

Earlier, when the man mentioned the name of the LORD, he started to see some hope (v. 18). Here the individual tries to do the same. Finding himself in deep trouble, he calls on the name of the LORD (v. 55). From the pit he cries out to the Lord: "hear my voice" (v. 56, my own translation).

Verses 55–57 are difficult to translate because of the complexity of the Hebrew perfect verb tense. Some of the verbs refer to an event that is fully in the past, while others imply that the situation is still continuing. So the question arises of whether the man is speaking about what God has done in the past, or what he wants him to do in the present. The grammatical arguments are complicated,[27] but I am inclined to agree with Provan, who translates verses 56–57 as follows: "Hear my voice! Do not close your ear to my gasping, my cry for help! Come near in the day when I call! Tell me not to be afraid!"[28]

After telling God what others have done to him (vv. 52–54), the individual now asks God to do something about his situation (vv. 56–57). *Pagsusumbong sa Diyos* (reporting to God) includes an expectation that God will do something for the individual, who on his own is incapable of changing the situation. He cries out to God to "look" at what his enemies have done to him: "the wrong done to me" (v. 59), "their vengeance (v. 60), "their

---

27. The main issue here is how to translate the perfect tense of the Hebrew verb because in some cases they act like the imperative. As Dobbs-Allsopp, *Lamentations*, 126, explains: "the verb form [of perfect] itself is very flexible and can take on different nuances depending on context . . . The interspersed presence throughout this section of actual imperatives ("do not close," 3:56; "do not fear," 3:57; "judge," 3:59; "see," 3:63) and of other volitive forms (3:64–66) . . . are broadly indicative of this latter (precative) use of the perfect." For a discussion of the "precative" perfect, see Iain W. Provan, "Past, Present and Future in Lamentations 3:52–66: The Case for a Precative Perfect Re-Examined," *VT* 41 (1991): 164–175.
28. Ibid., 174.

insults" (v. 61), "what my enemies whisper . . . against me all day long" (v. 62), how they mock him (v. 63). In the light of all these, he utters what is called an imprecatory prayer (see Imprecatory Prayer as *Pagsusumbong sa Diyos*, pp. 88–90). He asks God to "pay them back what they deserve" (v. 64), put a curse on them (v. 65), and "destroy them" (v. 66).

THE IMPRECATORY PRAYER AS *PAGSUSUMBONG SA DIYOS* (TELLING GOD ABOUT THE WRONG DONE TO US)[1]

In several places in Lamentations we find prayers that God will punish the speaker's enemies (see 1:21–22; 3:61–66; 4:21–22). Traditionally, such prayers are called "imprecatory prayers," in the same way that prayers on behalf of others are called "intercessory prayers." The difference is that the imprecatory psalm is a prayer against someone or a particular group of people. It is a petition to God that something bad or evil will happen to our enemies, whom we see as wicked.

While an imprecatory prayer is similar to what we know as curse, it is not exactly the same as a curse. When we curse and wish someone to be struck by lightning (*tamaan sana siya ng kidlat*) we are close to what is called imprecatory prayer. But when we make an imprecatory prayer, we are not simply wishing that something bad will happen to someone, we are asking God to make it happen.

Here are examples of imprecatory prayers in the book of Psalms:

- "Break the arm of the wicked man; call the evildoer to account for his wickedness that would not otherwise be found out." (Ps 10:15)

- "Rise up, LORD, confront them, bring them down; with your sword rescue me from the wicked." (Ps 17:13)

- "May those who seek my life be disgraced and put to shame; may those who plot my ruin be turned back in dismay." (Ps 35:4)

- "Let death take my enemies by surprise; let them go down alive to the realm of the dead, for evil finds lodging among them." (Ps 55:15)

- "May they be blotted out of the book of life and not be listed with the righteous." (Ps 69:28)

- "Daughter Babylon, doomed to destruction, happy is the one who repays you according to what you have done to us. Happy is the one who seizes your infants and dashes them against the rocks." (Ps 137:8–9)

How should we understand these prayers as Christians? How should we pray them? Or should we pray them at all?

---

1. Adapted from Federico Villanueva, *Psalms 1–72*, 274–276.

Some think that Christians cannot pray such harsh and violent prayers, and that those who do so are sinning. In some lectionaries, some of the words of the imprecatory psalms have been deleted. But before we judge these prayers as sinful or evil, we need to remember that they have been preserved in the Holy Scriptures. There must be a reason why God has allowed them to be part of our Bible.

All of us will agree that it is better to ask God to punish the wicked than to do it yourself. Those praying the imprecatory prayers are not taking the law into their own hands. Rather, they are bringing the matter to God, who is the righteous judge. They are being honest to God about what they truly feel. They are real. One of the problems we have today is that we have become too nice – so much so that once when I was really annoyed by something that happened in a church, a church leader was shocked that pastors get annoyed!

As followers of Jesus we are commanded to love even our enemies. But we know that this is far from easy. Yet some Christians deny that they are angry and claim that they simply forgive those who have done them wrong. But there is something wrong with forgiving too soon. Unless our emotions are properly dealt with, they may simply be suppressed. We may think we have forgiven someone when all we have done is deny our anger. Because of the desire to move on, we can rush through the process and in the end find ourselves even angrier than before.

The imprecatory psalms allow us to be human, to admit that we are angry. This is a humbling experience. It is not easy to admit to the Lord that actually we do not love our enemies but instead wish them destroyed. But that is better than denying it, for the Lord knows our heart anyway. So why deny the truth?

The imprecatory prayers should be understood within the context of the justice of God. They are expressions of hope in the God who is utterly just and righteous. We long for justice, but we know that many times justice is denied to those who need it most. Human justice is very imperfect. In many parts of Asia, victims do not have the power or the means to secure even a hearing.

The imprecatory psalms can best be understood within our context through the Filipino concept of *pagsusumbong*. It refers to someone who is weak or vulnerable going to someone in authority to "report" some injustice and appeal for some action in response. But you do not just make *sumbong* (report) to anyone, only to people you trust (e.g. your own father). You make *sumbong* because you believe the person to whom you are speaking has your best interest at heart. You also trust that this person has the power to redress the injustice. Viewed this way, the imprecatory prayers become expressions of trust in God our Father who is not only powerful but is also just and loving. They bring comfort to those who are weak and oppressed, who have no one else to go to but God. They also serve as a strong warning to oppressors. There is a God who fights for the right of the weak.

The imprecatory prayers thus form an important part of the life of the worshiping community. Writing about their use in Psalms, Zenger has this to say:

> [These psalms] uncover the mechanisms of violence as actions and strategies emanating from concrete human beings and institutions . . . These psalms can and will make obvious the web of violence presented, especially for the weak, the suffering, and those under attack . . . With their concrete expressions of fear and pain, they bring that pain to the center of ordinary religious and social life. They are the expression of that sensitivity to suffering that is constitutive for biblical piety, and for any way of life that is shaped by the Bible.[2]

When issues of justice are no longer mentioned in the prayers of God's people, they cease to be an issue of prime importance and gets pushed aside, and neglected. To cry out once more before God that something is not right falls in line with the justice of God, who will one day come to judge the living and the dead.

---

2. Zenger, *A God of Vengeance? Understanding the Psalms of Divine Wrath*, 74–75.

LAMENTATIONS 4

Once you have reached rock bottom, the only way to go is up. In Lamentations 4 the people feel that "our end had come" (4:18). Like the man in 3:18 they are without hope. They have seen the worst transpire before their very eyes – mothers eating their own children (4:10). Nothing worse can happen than that. The prophet Isaiah had asked: "Can a mother forget the baby at her breast and have no compassion on the child she has borne?" (Isa 49:15). The answer in Lamentations is "yes, she can, and even worse." We would agree with the poet: "The LORD has given full vent to his wrath" (v. 11). Yet it is at the point when God has exhausted his anger that the people also start to see some hope, so that the last verse of the chapter declares: "Your punishment will end, Daughter Zion" (v. 22).

For those undergoing extreme suffering, Lamentations 4 is a reminder that often it is when we think we have experienced the worst that the end is near. Those who have gone through long bouts of depression know that sometimes it is in the darkest night that one can see the smallest glimmer of light.

At the same time, Lamentations teaches us that the road to restoration may be long. Even the poetic form of Lamentations 4 conveys a sense of exhaustion. Like the previous three chapters, it is an acrostic. But whereas in Lamentations 1 and 2 three lines were allocated to each letter of the Hebrew alphabet, and in Lamentations 3 three verses were allocated to each letter, now in Lamentations 4, each letter is assigned a mere two lines. This repeated use of an acrostic structure means that we cycle through the issues from a to z and then go back again to the beginning. The pattern implies that resolution cannot be achieved in one go. It is a long process that takes time. But after three such cycles, fatigue sets in. The process of mourning that started in Lamentations 1 has gone a long way, but will the poet still have the strength and the energy to carry on? The change to a two-line acrostic structure suggests that his strength is flagging.

But while the poetic form shows sign of tiredness, the poet perseveres and does not change his subject matter: "Chapter Four is a sustained, eye-witness account of the siege and fall of the city told in the third person."[1] The fact that the poet is able to sustain and even intensify the narrating of the story

---

1. Mintz, "Rhetoric of Lamentations, 2.

demonstrates a persistence that we seldom see in our world today, where everything and everyone is in a hurry. After the tension between lament and praise in chapter 3, we are back to the situation of lament as the poet for the last time recalls the dreadful events when Jerusalem fell. It has taken three chapters to prepare us for this.

4:1–11 THE POET MOURNS AGAIN THE FALL OF JERUSALEM

The very first word in verse 1 is the same as in chapters 1 and 2. All three chapters begin with the funeral cry – *eikha* (see 1:1):

- 1:1 *How* lonely sits the city that was full of people! (ESV)
- 2:1 *How* the Lord has covered Daughter Zion with the cloud of his anger!
- 4:1 *How* the gold has lost its luster, the fine gold become dull!
- 4:2 *How* the precious children of Zion, once worth their weight in gold, are now considered as pots of clay.[2]

Here we notice that in chapter 4 the cry *eikha* is heard not just once, as in the first two chapters, but twice, a clear progression. Grief is a process. And sometimes, rather than diminishing, it intensifies. One does not lament a loss quickly, especially if what was lost is precious. It takes time for someone like the mother who lost her husband and two small children or the father who lost twenty-two members of his family in Typhoon Yolanda to grieve. There will be repeated moments when like the poet they will cry, *eikha* or its equivalent ("*ay*" among the Ilokanos).

When we are confronted with a tragedy such as the loss of a loved one, we need to avoid two extremes. The first is getting stuck in our grief, no longer even wanting to move on. Part of the beauty of the book of Lamentations is that there is some form in the lament. The acrostic structure means that we are forced to move forward even while trying to grieve every loss and every pain. The acrostic structure also reminds us there is an end, though the process may take some time. That is why it is a brilliant idea to have a series of five chapters rather than one long chapter. We all need some time to pause and to rest.

---

2. In Hebrew, v. 2 begins with "sons of Zion," not *eikha* ("how"), though the NIV translation may very well represent the sense of v. 2. The employment of the acrostic may have been responsible for the appearance of *eikha* in the second line.

The second extreme to be avoided is that of rushing towards resolution. In the fast-paced world in which we now live, we are prone to rush many things, including mourning. There used to be a time when people would devote days and even months to the period of mourning. Now people try to move on as quickly as possible. We tend to deny ourselves the necessary space for proper mourning. The pressure of the things that constantly call for our attention tempts us to ignore our pain. We postpone. We push our issues to the backstage where nobody can see them. We supress what we feel, tagging it as negative. In our attempt to show others we are in control, we fake even our smile. Until it is too late.

Not so with the poet. He takes time to linger on the pain and his memories. At first glance, it appears that he is lamenting the same things as in the previous chapters: the loss of former glory and present suffering. For instance, in chapter 1, he laments that the city which was once "great among the nations" has become a slave (v. 1). In chapter 2, the poet cries out: "How the Lord has . . . hurled down the splendor of Israel from heaven to earth" (v. 1). Likewise, in Lamentations 4, he speaks of precious stones that are now scattered in the streets. Three Hebrew words for gold are used in verses 1–2: *zahab* ("gold"), *ketem tov* ("fine gold"), and *paz* ("gold"). As indicated by the translation, "sacred gems" in v. 1, the gold referred to may have come from the temple that was burnt down by the Babylonians (see v. 11 which speaks of the Lord kindling a "fire in Zion"). But it is more likely that verse 1 and verse 2 are meant to be parallel, so that what is being referred to is not the literal gold in the temple but the once glorious people of Zion, referred to as "the precious children of Zion." The same Hebrew word translated "street corner" in verse 1 is repeated in verses 5, 8, 14. It reminds us of the fate of the children who "faint from hunger at every street corner" (2:19). Often, it is when something or someone is gone that we realize the value of what we have lost.

On closer examination, we see that although the poet is still lamenting the same experience, there is a different texture to his words. In Lamentations 4, he focuses on what has become of his people. Those who were once "precious" have become worse than the despised jackals. At least jackals "offer their breasts to nurse their young, but my people have become heartless" (v. 3). The previous chapters presented the cruelty of God (see 2:1–8; 3:1–18); now the emphasis is on the cruelty of mothers. The "children beg for bread" but are given none (4:3). Rather than giving food to their children, the mothers have cooked and eaten their children (v. 10). They were driven to this horrific act by the torments of hunger and thirst (see vv. 4–5). The poet considers death by starvation worse than death by the sword: "Those killed by the sword are better off than those who die of famine" (v. 9). At least death by sword is quick, unlike the prolonged agony of starvation, and it does not produce the horrible temptation to commit crimes like that of the mothers.

The poet considers the punishment of the people of Jerusalem "greater than that of Sodom" (v. 6). "Throughout the Old Testament the destruction of Sodom (and Gomorrah) was regarded as the ultimate in divine judgment (cf. for instance Amos 4:11)."[3] So the poet is saying that the punishment his people have endured goes beyond the worst possible punishment. Death in Sodom came quickly, unlike the protracted suffering in Judah. Implicit here is the complaint of Lady Zion: "Is any suffering like my suffering that was inflicted on me, that the LORD brought on me in the day of his fierce anger?" (Lam 1:12).

Mothers eating their own children is the worst possible scenario after a disaster. It is almost unheard of. As Paul Swarup comments: "Many South Asian mothers living in abject poverty have killed their children and themselves rather than watching them die like this."[4] In the Philippines, we have heard of a mother who set her children on fire, but that was because she was mentally ill. We have also heard of a child committing suicide apparently because of her poverty.[5] But we do not hear of mothers eating their own children. This is an unthinkable aberration from the sacrificial love of mothers. We hope that the poet is using poetic exaggeration rather than recounting what actually happened. But if it did happen, then indeed, "the Lord has given full vent to his wrath" (v. 11). Nothing could be worse than this. This is the lowest point possible to reach. The people are justified in saying that God has destroyed the "foundations" of Zion (v. 11).

Care for our own is basic to our humanity; when even this is taken from us, the end has indeed come. God has exhausted his anger (see v. 11). What can be left after his people have been driven to such extremities?

---

3. Robert B. Salters, *Jonah and Lamentations* (Sheffield: JSOT Press, 1994), 113.
4. Swarup, "Lamentations," 1023.
5. Online: http://www.philstar.com/headlines/26165/poverty-drives-girl-commit-suicide (accessed March 29, 2016).

4:12–18 "OUR END HAD COME"

Verse 12 does not refer to the atrocities spoken of above, but it does make it clear that it was the actions of their enemies that led to this situation. People who heard about what happened to Jerusalem could not believe it. The city that the psalmist said would never be moved has fallen. An enemy had actually entered Jerusalem and destroyed it (v. 12).

The question the people are now asking is "Why did God allow this to happen to us?"[6] As in the previous chapters, there is an attempt to make sense of their tragic experience (compare 1:5, 8; 2:14). The explanation is similar to the one given in 2:14, though in this case it is more explicit: it is because of the sins of the prophets and the priests (4:12).

What a heavy responsibility spiritual leaders carry! They are the ones who should be declaring to the people what the Lord requires. But often it is easier to proclaim what people want to hear, especially when the Lord's message is not popular or even contradicts the popular view. We all know how easy it is to just go with the flow, without realizing that as spiritual leaders our actions and inaction will eventually lead to the people's destruction.

The prophet Jeremiah lamented that the prophets and the priests had failed in treating the already serious wound of his people: "They have treated the wound[7] carelessly, when they say 'Peace, peace,' when there is no peace" (Jer 8:11). It was thus the prophets and the priests "who shed within her the blood of the righteous" (v. 13). Again we are reminded of the great responsibility that lay on the shoulders of the spiritual leaders. The survival, indeed the very existence, of the people was dependent not on the stability of the status quo but on the Lord (see vv. 17–18 below). The spiritual leaders were the ones who were supposed to be "righteous." Instead, they are now guilty of shedding the "blood of the righteous."

It is not clear exactly who "the righteous" are whose blood has been shed (v. 13). The poet may be referring to the children "who faint from hunger at every street corner" (2:19). Similarly, the ones referred to as "righteous" in chapter 4 now "grope through the streets as if they were blind" (4:14). But the context of verses 14–15 points to a more general reference. So does the description of people covered with so much blood that others view them as

---

6. The shift to first person plural pronouns in vv. 17–20 shows that the poet is presenting the view of the people or speaking on their behalf.
7. The word translated "wound" (*sheber*) is the same word used in Lamentations to speak of the destruction of the city (Lam 2:11; 4:10). The word also means "break/fracture."

unclean, like lepers. They have become like the unwanted refugees today, who arrive in boats begging to be received but are rejected at the borders.

Most painful of all, it is the Lord himself who has "scattered them" (v. 16). Verse 16 continues, "he no longer shows regard for them" (my own translation). The word translated "show regard" comes from the same verb translated "look" when Lady Zion begged God to look at her situation (see 1:11). The people's experience has taught them that God is no longer listening to them. Like Lady Zion they are hurt by God's action. We see this in the way they treat the priests: "The priests are shown no honor" (v. 16). When someone hurts us, our relationship with those who are close to that person are also affected. In the case of Lamentations, the people are unable to give vent to their sense of having been hurt by God, and so they express their feelings by the way they treat God's representatives, the priests.

Because they feel that the Lord is no longer looking after them, the people look for help from other nations. The psalmist spoke of lifting "my eyes to the mountains – where does my help come from?" (Ps 121:1). In the same way, the people looked for help: "from our towers we watched for a nation that could save us" (Lam 4:17). But they soon realized that the nation they were expecting to save them could not do so. They had been hoping that the Egyptians would drive off the Babylonians, but their hopes were dashed.

When people are desperate, they tend to pin their hopes on someone or some other nation, only to be let down by this "vain" hope. We experience this all the time when we are in trouble. We are tempted to put our trust in our fellow human being rather than on God. And when we do, we realize the same thing that the people did in Lamentations: the situation remains the same – "People stalked us at every step, so we could not walk in our streets" (v. 18). They continue to feel helpless in the face of their enemies (v. 19). Even their very own king, the "LORD's anointed" whom they consider "our very life breath" was taken away from them (v. 20). The specific historical event being referred to here was the capture of King Zedekiah by the Babylonians (2 Kgs 25:1–7). No wonder the people despaired and felt that "our end had come" (v. 18).

4:21–22 SUDDEN CHANGE OF MOOD

Yet precisely at this point of despair, we are startled by the sudden change of mood in the instruction in verse 21 – "Rejoice." But this is a bitter joy, for this command is not directed to Zion but to Edom. The Edomites were half-brothers of the people of Judah through their common ancestors Abraham and Isaac. So they would have been expected to help Judah. But the Edomites turned their backs on them during one of the most difficult times of their history. Here "Daughter Edom" represents their enemies.

Although there is no direct prayer in Lamentations 4, it is safe to assume that the imprecatory prayers uttered in the previous chapters are still relevant here (see 3:64–66). The people somehow know that God has heard them. Thus, like the psalmist, they can now turn to their enemies and say "away from me" (Ps 6:8). In Lamentations 4, they go even further and utter a curse in the form of a taunt – "Rejoice . . . Edom . . . to you also the cup will be passed" (v. 21). The cup refers to the cup of punishment.

After all they have gone through, the poet feels that the punishment of the people has now come to an end. He addresses Lady Zion: "The punishment of your iniquity, O daughter of Zion, is accomplished" (v. 22, ESV). The word translated "accomplished" also means "complete." The punishment of Edom has yet to start, but the punishment of Judah is over.

LAMENTATIONS 5

One of the central themes in the final chapter of Lamentations is community. Suffering has a way of bringing people together. I saw this firsthand when Typhoon Ondoy inundated our village. The neighborhood instantly turned into a community. The flooding made us vulnerable. Those whom I knew by sight but had never spoken to became companions as we queued together to get clean water from a neighbor's well. There is overwhelming evidence showing that being in a community facilitates recovery during times of disaster.

Recovery or restoration is another theme in Lamentations 5. The movement from isolation (Lam 1) to community (Lam 5) signals the way to recovery. The book opened with the voice of a lone narrator who mourned the destruction of the city, personified as a woman sitting "alone," weeping. She complains that there is no one to comfort her. In traditional Asian cultures, this is a double tragedy. The destruction of Jerusalem is terrible, but to suffer alone is unbearable. The statement that pain "can only be experienced by individuals"[1] is not true for everyone.[2] As Lamentations 5 demonstrates, pain can also be experienced by an entire community together.

But in order to move to a place of healing, it is not enough just to form a community or to be in community. Our need is not just social; it is also spiritual. A community needs God. What makes the community in Lamentations different from some of the communities we see today is that it is a community in prayer. They recognize that genuine restoration has to have restoration to God at its center. This can be seen in the overall structure of the prayer:

- Petition: "Remember, LORD, what has happened to us" (v. 1)
- Lament: Detailed description of what has happened to them (vv. 2–18)
- Lament: "Why?" (vv. 19–21)
- Petition: "Restore us to yourself" (v. 21)

The last prayer of the people is a plea to God: "Restore us to yourself, LORD" (v. 21). Restoration is ultimately a restoration of our relationship with God. It certainly involves physical, psychological, and emotional elements.

---

1. Heim, "Personification of Jerusalem," 130, following Mintz, "Rhetoric of Lamentations," 2.
2. This may be something many Westerners have forgotten as a result of the strong emphasis on the individual. As Brueggemann admits: "we have yet to learn in any way about grief as a public practice" (Walter Brueggemann, *Hopeful Imagination* [Philadelphia, PA: Fortress, 1986], 33).

But for restoration to be holistic, it has to include the spiritual. Without a real change in the people's relationship with God, no change will last.

5:1 PETITION: "REMEMBER, LORD, WHAT HAS HAPPENED TO US"

Lamentations 5 differs from the previous chapters in that it is a communal voice that speaks and in that it does not have an acrostic structure. True, it has 22 verses, which matches the 22 letters of the Hebrew alphabet, but it is not bound by the order in which these letters appear in the alphabet. Thus, we may say that here the poet has more freedom in organizing the ideas, or the prayer.

While the other chapters do contain prayers, these are interspersed with dramatized speech. By contrast, Lamentations 5 is all prayer. By ending the book in this manner, all that has gone before is transformed, as it were, into a culminating act of prayer. Everything, every conversation, every speech, including the things said about God and the complaints uttered – all become a prayer to the Lord.

The opening verse is a prayer of petition. This also is a development. In the previous chapters the petition usually came at the end (2:20–22; 3:64–66) or in the middle (1:9, 11). The fourth chapter does not contain any petition. So in a sense the short petitions in chapters 1–3 and the absence of petition in chapter 4 are remedied by the prayer in the last chapter.

The petition is for God to "remember." The "man" made a similar petition in chapter 3: "Remember my affliction" (3:19, ESV). Here in Lamentations 5, the whole community are crying out to God to "remember . . . what has happened to us" (v. 1a). It is not that God has literally forgotten them, for here remembering does not simply refer to an intellectual state. To call on God to remember is to ask him to act, do something in behalf of the petitioner. For example, when "God remembered" in Genesis 8:1, the waters began to recede (Gen 8:3; see also Gen 19:29). When God remembers, he does something; he acts.

But there is an added element to the petition "remember" in Lamentations 5. It indicates a sense of desperation. By this time, everyone has said her or his piece. Complaints have been aired. Cries have been uttered. Feelings of hurt have been shared with others and with God. The petition, "remember," is equivalent to Lady Zion's own plea, "Look, O LORD, and see" (1:11, ESV). The community praying used the same words: "look, and see" (5:1b). If in chapter 1, the community is personified as a woman, here the community itself is speaking. There is an element of directness this time. It took five chapters to reach this point.[3] But once it starts, it becomes like rain; it pours. In the next verses the people tell God one by one the things that have happened to them.

5:2–18 "WHAT HAS HAPPENED TO US"

Like a child reporting something that has happened to her mother,[4] the people tell God that their "inheritance has been turned over to strangers" (v. 2a). The word "inheritance" recalls the promise God made to their ancestors to give them the land. But this gift came with a condition: they would only remain in the land if they were faithful to the covenant. Since they have not been faithful, God has allowed their enemies to enter their land and do as they please. The passive form of the verb "has been turned over" points to the action of God and implies that the sin committed by the people is the cause of their suffering. As in the previous chapters, the people are aware of their culpability (see vv. 7, 16). But this did not prevent them from coming to God to tell him about what has happened to them. Mercy precedes repentance.

The people now become even more specific as they recite their griefs. When their enemies took their land, many of them lost not only their homes (v. 2b) but also their loved ones: "We have become fatherless, our mothers are widows" (v. 3). They feel orphaned. As they sought to find someone who could comfort them, they found God. They come to him because they believe he is "a father to the fatherless, a defender of widows" (Ps 68:5).

As fatherless children and widows, they became strangers in their own land, so much so that they have to buy the water they drink (v. 4a). Even the wood they use has to be bought at a price (v. 4b). This is the continuing story in my own country, where neo-colonialism means that foreigners continue to control the economy and exert influence in other areas of national life.

The continuing subjugation to their enemies has taken a toll on the people of Judah. They are "weary and find no rest" (v. 5). They would have known how our Filipino ancestors felt when they finally shook off more than 300 years of Spanish rule only to find themselves under a new master when

---

3. This approach is not unique to Judah, but is also found in our own culture. Our preferred way of communicating is indirect. We do not readily say what we want. We beat around the bush. Or as we say, *marami munang pasakalye* (there is lots of introduction).
4. In Filipino we call this *pagsusumbong*.

the Americans took over. Because of continuing poverty, many of our *kaba-bayan* are forced to leave their families to seek work, leaving a fatherless and motherless generation. Those working abroad know what Lamentations 5 is saying. Many of them are tired physically, psychologically, and emotionally.

Just to survive and get food to eat, the Israelites have "submitted to Egypt and Assyria" (v. 6). They suffer extreme hunger (v. 10) and have to risk their lives to find anything to eat (v. 9). All of them have suffered greatly. Their women have been raped (v. 11). Their "princes have been hung up by their hands" (a posture that may represent surrender) and their "elders are shown no respect" (v. 12). Their young men "toil at the millstones'" their "boys stagger under loads of wood" (v. 13). Their elders have given up their roles as leaders. The "gate" (v. 14) is the place where community decisions were made, but now there is no one there. Even the young men no longer sing their songs.

As the elders have ceased (*shabat*) coming to the gates, so "joy is gone (*shabat*) from our hearts" (v. 15a). The city that was called "the joy of the whole earth" (Lam 2:15) has now abandoned its singing. In contrast to the psalmist who declared how God "turned my wailing into dancing" (Ps 30:11), the people lament, "our dancing has turned to mourning" (Lam 5:15).

Alluding to their experience of "disgrace" (v. 1), they declare, "The crown has fallen from our head." They can only cry, "Woe to us, for we have sinned!" (v. 16). This is the second time in this chapter that the people admit their sins. In verse 7, they spoke about the sins of their ancestors and how they are bearing "their punishment." This does not mean that the people do not acknowledge their own sin. That much is clear from verse 16. Rather, their confessions show that they understand the corporate nature of sin (the sins of the parents affect the children – Neh 1:6) and also know that they themselves have sinned. Their continuing suffering is interpreted as an indication of their participation in the sins of their fathers. The sins of the spiritual leaders (priests and prophets) are also blamed for the sufferings of the people (Lam 4:13). But in crying out, "we have sinned," the people also admit they too bear guilt.

Many of the things the people tell God in verses 2–18 have already been mentioned in the previous chapters. For instance, the turning over of their inheritance to strangers (5:2) was mentioned in the first chapter (1:10). The struggle to find bread and the experience of hunger (5:9–10) were also stressed in 1:11 (which says the people are groaning "as they search for bread"). The failure to find rest (5:5) and the violence against women (5:11) find parallels in 1:3 and 1:10, respectively.

Why repeat these things to God?

First, the repetition reminds us of the continuing suffering of the people. They have been suffering for some time now and have still not received any answer. That is why they cry out to God, "Why do you forsake us so long?" (v. 20). Chapter 5 reveals the reality of the situation years after the destruction of their city. The repetition also tells us of the perseverance of the people – no matter how long they have suffered and cried out to God, they will never give up until God responds (see 3:49–50). It reminds us of the parable of the persistent widow who kept coming back to the judge until he agreed to hear her case. They are crying out to God because they continue to hope he will hear them. As Jesus tells his disciples, "And will not God bring about justice for his chosen ones, who cry out to him day and night?" (Luke 18:7).

Lastly, the people repeat the things that have happened to them because they believe these things matter to God. Otherwise, they would not make the effort to name them one by one. They believe that God is concerned not only with what happened to them but also with what they feel. That is why they tell God "we are weary and find no rest" (v. 5). And towards the end of their prayer, they admit to God that "our hearts are faint" (v. 17).[5] No matter how difficult the situation may be, as long as you have courage and inner strength you are able to continue. But once the heart grows faint, you are in trouble. There is no longer any motivation. No reason for continuing. From a human point of view, you are done.

5:19–22 "RESTORE US TO YOURSELF, LORD"

The good thing is that there is someone beyond the community to whom they can go. The people may be weary and faint, but God is not: "You, Lord, reign forever; your throne endures from generation to generation" (v. 19). Yet, immediately after telling God that he reigns forever, they lament: "Why do you always forget us? Why do you forsake us so long?" (v. 20).

I remember a time when I felt down and weary. It was towards the end of my PhD studies. The difficulty of life in a foreign land, the rigor of study, family problems – all of these had taken their toll. I was attending vespers and the congregation were singing a song that declares that God never grow

---

5. In Filipino this is translated as *pinanghihinaan na kami ng loob*.

weary. I found it hard to identify with the words of the song. I sat down and wept. "God," I said, "you never grow weary. But I am tired. I can't carry on any longer." I didn't receive any answer from God. But I felt relieved as I sensed within me that it is alright for me to admit I am tired. Just like the people in Lamentations, it is okay to pour out our hearts to God (see Lam 2:19).

The wonderful thing about God is that he understands us. He knows we are but dust (Ps 103:14). That is why he allows us to express ourselves to him, including our questions. Some may find the laments in the book of Lamentations shocking. How dare the people question God? Surely it's not true that God has forsaken them. Why would we question God? Has he not promised that he will never leave us nor forsake us (Heb 13:5)? Yet we also know that our Lord himself uttered the same cry on the cross when he said, "My God, my God, why have you forsaken me?" Rather than getting entangled with theologizing, the text invites us to sit with the people and mourn with them. For even though they are lamenting against God, they never let go of him. Almost in the same breath as their "why?" they pray, "Restore us to yourself, LORD, that we may return" (v. 21). Lament does not turn us away from God; it brings us closer to him.

Prayer for restoration reminds us that true healing and restoration ultimately leads to a restoration of one's life in God. Without restoration to God that results in moral transformation, there is no true restoration. Restoration is holistic, involving the physical, emotional, and the spiritual. The petition, "restore us to yourself," shows that the primary concern of the people is their relationship with God. They know that true restoration and healing can only come when God sees them from heaven (see 3:50). For true restoration to occur, the emphasis on spirituality should continue, not just in the initial stage of a disaster but throughout the whole process and beyond.

Studies show that spirituality is the number one coping mechanism of Filipinos who experience disaster. Consequently "making community spiritual activities part of the reconstruction and rehabilitation efforts has yielded positive effects."[6] There is a need to emphasize this because many Western organizations who come to the Philippines to do aid work do not give room for the religious or the spiritual in their approach and because "not all mental health and psychosocial service providers integrate this dimension in their

---

6. Lourdes Ladrido-Ignacio, "Basic Framework: Transformation of Victims of Disasters to Survivors," in *Ginhawa: Well-being in the Aftermath of Disasters*, 47

work."[7] With the growing secular environment in some parts of Asia, even the mentioning of God is sometimes prohibited. Yet such approaches will surely be found wanting in many parts of Asia where religion is central to life.

Though God never speaks in Lamentations,[8] yet he is very much present in the conversations and speeches throughout the book. He is the one talked about and complained to. In later Rabbinic writings such as the one we find in Lamentations Rabbati, God becomes the main speaker of the words of Lamentations as God himself weeps for the sufferings of Lady Zion. In its attempt to provide hope and encouragement the overall direction of Lamentations was transformed by presenting it as the lament of God over the destruction of Jerusalem and the suffering which he himself has inflicted upon his people.[9]

Such a view of God is reflected in Lamentations 5. Even when the people lament against God, he remains the one to whom the people go. Even when there is no answer, the people continue to cling to God. The very last verse in Lamentations 5, the last verse in the whole book, is full of uncertainty – "unless you have utterly rejected us and are angry with us beyond measure" (v. 22).

This verse is controversial because some scholars feel it is an "inappropriate" ending. "The translation of Lamentations 5 verse 22 poses a problem to exegetes and translators. This is the case not so much because the words or the construction are obscure; rather, it is a case of what is an appropriate close for the poem."[10] Indeed, the arguments supporting particular views are based on what each scholar considers an "appropriate" ending. Some feel that translating the Hebrew word, *ki 'im* as "but" or "unless" makes the ending too negative. So they propose other readings, for example, "even though."[11] While this rendering is possible on grammatical grounds, we should not dismiss the other alternative on the basis of its appropriateness. Who decides what is an appropriate ending? Is a negative ending automatically inappropriate? The power of Lamentations lies in its capacity to hold the tension between faith and doubt. Faith and doubt go together; in fact, doubt strengthens faith.

7. Ibid., 64.
8. We have heard many different speakers in the book, but we have never heard the voice of God.
9. Shaye J. D. Cohen, "The Destruction: From Scripture to Midrash," *Prooftexts* 2 (1982): 18–39.
10. I. G. P. Gous, "Lamentations 5 and the Translation of Verse 22," *OTE* 3 (1990): 287.
11. Robert Gordis, "Conclusion of the Book of Lamentations (5:22)," *JBL* 93, no. 2 (1974): 291–293.

The ending is also relevant in our own situation where there is so much uncertainty. In a society where everything is predictable, the ending of Lamentations 5 may be disturbing. But where almost everything (including traffic!) is unpredictable, the negative ending is liberating! We are not alone. It is okay to end on a negative note, at least for the time being. The book of Lamentations has to be read in the light of the entire Scriptures which contains the answer and a message of hope.[12] But there are situations when we need Lamentations 5:22 in order to survive.

---

12. Wright, *Message of Lamentations*, 56.

COMMUNAL LAMENT AND THE ASIAN CONTEXT

Lament is an expression of one's questions, feelings of hurt, and complaints to God. It is the pouring out of one's heart to God. The main goal is that through this act one's relationship with God will grow and deepen, both personally and communally.

Scholars group the laments in the Bible into two main categories – individual laments and communal laments. The former concerns the experience of an individual and make much use of the personal pronoun "I" (see for example, Pss 3, 6, and 13), though in some cases the "I" represents the community. The communal lament is dominated by the experience of the community as indicated by the first personal plural pronouns "we" or "us" (see Pss 44 and 89). Lamentations 5 is an example of a communal lament.

A more significant distinction between individual and communal laments lies in the latter's capacity to handle ambiguity and the elements that are in tension. Individual laments often move from lament to praise (see Ps 13), but this is not the case in communal laments. Most of the communal laments end without any clear resolution or positive note. Lamentations 5 is the classic example. This chapter ends without any resolution as the people asks God, "Why do you always forget us? Why do you forsake us so long?" (5:20). The last two verses contain a petition, with a note of uncertainty: "Restore us to yourself, LORD that we may return; renew our days as of old unless you have utterly rejected us and are angry with us beyond measure" (5:21–22). That is how the chapter, and thus the whole book of Lamentations end. The tension remains unresolved, the question unanswered.

It can even be said that whereas in the Psalms most individual laments move from lament to praise, the direction is reversed in communal laments. There the movement is from praise to lament. It's almost like the praise is meant to emphasize the lament. Two examples will suffice. The first is Psalm 44. This psalm is divided into two main sections – praise (vv. 1–8) and lament (vv. 9–26). The first part begins with a recitation of the great things that God has done culminating in the declaration, "In God we make our boast all day long, and we will praise your name forever" (v. 8). But this is immediately followed by a strong contrastive statement: "But now you have rejected and humbled us; you no longer go out with our armies" (v. 9). The lament portion contains a complaint and petition similar to the one in Lamentations 5: "Why do you hide your face and forget our misery and oppression?" (Ps 44:24). The last verse is a petition with no clear resolution: "Rise up and help us; rescue us because of your unfailing love" (v. 26).

Psalm 89 is the longer version of Psalm 44. The first part is clearly thanksgiving (vv. 1–38). It begins with the words, "I will sing of the LORD's great love forever" (v. 1). The psalmist recalls the great things that he has done and God's faithfulness. But this long thanksgiving is followed by a long lament beginning with verse 39: "But you have rejected, you have spurned, you have been very angry with your anointed one." The people ask God, "How long, LORD? Will you hide yourself forever? How long will your wrath burn like fire?" (v. 46).

This capacity to face uncertainty, tension, and even doubt characterizes the communal lament as we see in the two psalms above and in Lamentations 5 (see also, Ps 74 and 79). Another feature that we observe in communal lament is the frankness or openness with which the people who utter them approach God. Asians in general may find it difficult to express their questions to God. This is partly because of our traditional value of respect. We do not question the elderly, how much less can we question God. Filipinos in general are also not assertive, although this is changing as a result of the influence Western values.

But I think these two elements in the communal lament – the capacity for embracing tension and openness to God – are crucial in our time. We live in the midst of many uncertainties. As I write this article, a mayor from Davao has just been elected as president. He is known for his killings, gutter language, and immoral lifestyle. Many say that his rise to power is an indication of the desperation of our people. Duterte has promised to end corruption and the drug problem in six months. But as one commentator wrote, without a clear vision and a platform for government, it is more likely that we are on the way to a road that is full of uncertainty.

It is in this sense that we can say the communal lament is God's gift for us. We all know that uncertainty is not easy, even unbearable if prolonged. But the communal lament demonstrates to us that when we are together we can face whatever lies ahead. As a community, we are not alone. We have each other, and we have God. The good news is that the God of the Bible is not like other leaders who cannot be questioned. He not only allows but encourages the pouring out of the hearts of his people. It might take a Moses or a David to confront God face to face. But for the rest of us, we need a community to face God. The communal lament empowers us to stand for what we believe is just and right. "If we cannot challenge the governance of this world, then we cannot challenge the governors of the world. The churches' unwillingness or incapacity to bring radical discontent, protest, and anger before God silences and denies reality. It teaches sheepishness, lying, and cowardice. Protest of injustice and oppression is learned in prayer."[1]

---

1. O'Connor, "The Book of Lamentations," in *The New Interpreter's Bible* Vol. 6, 1044.

BIBLIOGRAPHY

Abrams, M. H., and Geoffrey Galt Harpham. *A Glossary of Literary Terms*. 10th ed. Boston, MA: Wadsworth, 2012.

Adeney-Risakotta, Bernard. "Is There a Meaning in Natural Disasters? Constructions of Culture, Religion, and Science." *Exchange* 38 (2009): 226–243.

Albrektson, Bertil. *Studies in the Text and Theology of Lamentations*. Vol. 21. Studia Theologica Lundensia. Lund: Gleerup, 1963.

Allen, Leslie C. *A Liturgy of Grief: A Pastoral Commentary on Lamentations*. Grand Rapids, MI: Baker, 2011.

Archer, John. *The Nature of Grief: The Evolution and Psychology of Reactions to Loss*. New York: Routledge, 1999.

Balentine, Samuel E. *The Hidden God: The Hiding of the Face of God in the Old Testament*. Oxford: Oxford University Press, 1983.

Bankoff, Greg. *Cultures of Disaster: Society and Natural Hazard in the Philippines*. London and New York: RoutledgeCurson, 2003.

Begrich, Joachim. "Das Priesterliche Heilsorakel." *ZAW* 52 (1934): 81–92.

Beltran, Benigno P. *The Christology of the Inarticulate: An Inquiry into the Filipino Understanding of Jesus the Christ*. Manila: Divine Word Publications, 1987.

Bergant, Dianne. "'êkāh: A Gasp of Desperation (Lamentations 1:1)." *Int* 67 (2013): 144–154.

Berlin, Adele. *Lamentations: A Commentary*. Louisville, KY: Westminster John Knox Press, 2002.

———. "On Writing a Commentary on Lamentations." In *Lamentations in Ancient and Contemporary Cultural Contexts*, edited by Nancy C. Lee and Carleen Mandolfo, 3–11. Atlanta, GA: Society of Biblical Literature, 2008.

———. "Psalms and the Literature of Exile: Psalms 137, 44, 69 and 78." In *The Book of Psalms: Composition and Reception*, edited by Peter W. Flint, Patrick D. Miller, Aaron Brunell, and Ryan Roberts, 65–86. Vol. 99 *VTSup*. Leiden, Boston: Brill, 2005.

Bier, Miriam J. "'Perhaps There Is Hope': Reading Lamentations as a Polyphony of Pain, Penitence, and Protest." A Thesis Submitted for the Degree of Doctor of Philosophy at the University of Otago, Dunedin, New Zealand, 2012.

Billman, Kathleen D. and Daniel L. Migliore. *Rachel's Cry: Prayer of Lament and Rebirth of Hope*. Cleveland, OH: United Church Press, 1999.

Boda, Mark J., Carol J. Dempsey, and LeAnn Snow Flesher. *Daughter Zion: Her Portrait, Her Response*. Atlanta, GA: SBL, 2012.

Brady, Christian M. M. *The Rabbinic Targum of Lamentations: Vindicating God*. Leiden, Boston: Brill, 2003.

Braiterman, Zachary. "Lamentations in Modern Jewish Thought." In *Great Is Thy Faithfulness?: Reading Lamentations as Sacred Scripture*, edited by Robin A. Parry and Heath Thomas, 92–97. Eugene, OR: Pickwick Publications, 2011.

Brueggemann, Walter. "Formfulness of Grief." *Int* 31, no. 3 (July 1977): 263–275.

———. *Hopeful Imagination: Prophetic Voices in Exile*. Philadelphia, PA: Fortress, 1986.

———. *The Message of the Psalms: A Theological Commentary*. Minneapolis, MN: Augsburg, 1984.

Capaque, George N. "The Problem of Evil in the Filipino Context." In *Doing Theology in the Philippines*, edited by John D. Suk, 99–116. Manila: Asian Theological Seminary; OMF Literature, 2005.

Clines, David J. A. "Job." In *New Bible Commentary*, edited by D. A. Carson, R. T. France, and G. J. Wenham, 459–84. Leicester: IVP, 1994.

Cohen, Shaye J. D. "The Destruction: From Scripture to Midrash." *Prooftexts* 2 (1982): 18–39.

Diamond, A. R. Pete and Kathleen M. O'Connor, "Unfaithful Passions: Coding Women Coding Men in Jeremiah 2–3," *BibInt* 4 (1996), 288–310.

Dobbs-Allsopp, F. W. "Tragedy, Tradition, and Theology in the Book of Lamentations." *JSOT* 74 (1997): 29–60.

———. *Weep, O Daughter of Zion: A Study of the City-Lament Genre in the Hebrew Bible*. Roma: Editrice Pontificio Istituto Biblico, 1993.

Foley, Helene P. *Female Acts in Greek Tragedy*. Princeton, NJ: Princeton University Press, 2001.

Francisco, Jose Mario C. "Panitikan at Kristiyanismong Pilipino: Ang Nagbabagong Larawan ni Kristo." *Philippine Studies* 25 (1977): 186–214.

Gaspar, Karl M. *Desperately Seeking God's Saving Action: Yolanda Survivors' Hope Beyond Heartbreaking Lamentations*. Quezon City, Philippines: Institute of Spirituality in Asia, 2014.

Golez, Rosana B., and Joel P. Garduce, eds. *Surges: Outpourings in Haiyan/Yolanda's Wake*. Makati City, Philippines: Rosana B. Golez and Joel P. Garduce, 2013.

Gottwald, Norman K. *Studies in the Book of Lamentations*. London: SCM Press, 1962.

Gordis, Robert. "Conclusion of the Book of Lamentations (5:22)." *JBL* 93 (1974): 289–293.

Gous, I. G. P. "Lamentations 5 and the Translation of Verse 22." *OTE* 3 (1990): 287–302.

Green, Ronald M. "Theodicy." In *The Encyclopedia of Religion*, edited by Mircea Eliade and Charles J. Adams, 430–441. Vol 14. New York: Macmillan, 1987.

Gunkel, Hermann. *Einleitung in die Psalmen die Gattungen der religiösen Lyrik Israels*. Göttingen: Vandenhoeck and Ruprecht, 1933.

———. *The Psalms: A Form-Critical Introduction*. Philadelphia, PA: Fortress, 1967.

Heim, Knut. "The Personification of Jerusalem and the Drama of Her Bereavement in Lamentations." In *Zion, City of Our God*, edited by Richard S. Hess and Gordon J. Wenham, 129–169. Grand Rapids, MI: Eerdmans, 1999.

Hillers, Delbert R. *Lamentations*. The Anchor Bible. Garden City, NY: Doubleday, 1992.

Kaiser, Barbara Bakke. "Poet as 'Female Impersonator': The Image of Daughter Zion as Speaker in Biblical Poems of Suffering." *Journal of Religion* 67.2 (1987): 164–182.

King, Philip D. *Surrounded by Bitterness: Image Schemas and Metaphors for Conceptualizing Distress in Classical Hebrew*. Eugene, OR: Pickwick Publications, 2012.

Kitamori, Kazo. *Theology of the Pain of God*. Richmond, VA: John Knox Press, 1965.

Kövecses, Zoltán, and Réka Benczes. *Metaphor a Practical Introduction*. Oxford/ New York: Oxford University Press, 2010.

Kramer, Samuel Noah. "Lamentation over the Destruction of Ur." In *ANET*, edited by James B. Pritchard, 455–463. Princeton, NJ: Princeton University Press, 1969.

Ladrido-Ignacio, Lourdes. "Basic Framework: Transformation of Victims of Disasters to Survivors." In *Ginhawa: Well-Being in the Aftermath of Disasters*, edited by Lourdes Ladrido-Ignacio, 39–53. Philippine Psychiatrists Association and World Association for Psychosocial Rehabilitation, 2011.

Lahoz, Presentacion. "The Dung-Aw, The Ilocano Dirge." *Ilocos Review* 2 (1970): 61–72.

Lakoff, George, and Mark Johnson. *Metaphors We Live By*. Chicago, IL: University of Chicago Press, 1980.

Lanahan, William F. "The Speaking Voice in the Book of Lamentations." *JBL* 93 (1974): 41–49.

Lee, Archie Chi Chung. "Lamentations." In *Global Bible Commentary*, edited by Daniel Patte and Teresa Okure, 226–233. Nashville, TN: Abingdon, 2004.

Lee, Nancy C. "The Singers of Lamentations: (A)Scribing (De)Claiming Poets and Prophets." In *Lamentations in Ancient and Contemporary Cultural Contexts*, edited by Nancy C. Lee and Carleen Mandolfo. Atlanta, GA: Society of Biblical Literature, 2008.

Levenson, Jon D. "Zion Traditions." *ABD* 6:1098–1102.

Maggay, Melba Padilla. "Haiyan Challenge." Philippines: Institute for Studies in Asian Church and Culture, December 1, 2013.

———. *Pahiwatig: Kagawiang Pangkomunikasyon ng Filipino*. Quezon City: Ateneo de Manila University Press, 2002.

Mandolfo, Carleen. *Daughter Zion Talks back to the Prophets: A Dialogic Theology of the Book of Lamentations*. Atlanta, GA: Society of Biblical Literature, 2007.

Mare, W. Harold. "Zion." *ABD* 6:1096–1097.

Mintz, Alan. "The Rhetoric of Lamentations and the Representation of Catastrophe." *Prooftexts* 2 (1982): 1–17.

O'Connor, Kathleen. "The Book of Lamentations." In *The New Interpreter's Bible*, VI: 1013–1072, 2001.

———. *Jeremiah: Pain and Promise*. Minneapolis, MN: Fortress, 2011.

———. *Lamentations and the Tears of the World*. Maryknoll, NY: Orbis, 2002.

Olyan, Saul M. *Biblical Mourning: Ritual and Social Dimensions*. Oxford/New York: Oxford University Press, 2004.

Parratt, John, ed. *An Introduction to Third World Theologies*. Cambridge, UK/New York: Cambridge University Press, 2004.

Provan, Iain W. *Lamentations*. London: Marshall Pickering/Grand Rapids, MI: Eerdmans, 1991.

———. "Past, Present and Future in Lamentations 3:52–66: The Case for a Precative Perfect Re-Examined." *VT* 41 (1991): 164–175.

Renkema, Johan. *Lamentations*. Leuven: Peeters, 1998.

Salters, Robert B. *Jonah & Lamentations*. Sheffield, England: *JSOT* Press, 1994.

———. *Lamentations. A Critical and Exegetical Commentary*. London: Continuum International Pub. Group, 2010.

Sarna, Nahum M. "Interchange of the Prepositions Beth and Min in Biblical Hebrew." *JBL* 78.4 (1959): 310–316.

Scarry, Elaine. *The Body in Pain: The Making and Unmaking of the World*. New York/Oxford University Press, 1985.

Slavitt, D. R. *The Book of Lamentations: A Meditation and Translation*. Baltimore, MD: John Hopkins, 2001.

Smith-Christopher, Daniel. "Reassessing the Historical and Sociological Impact of the Babylonian Exile." In *Exile: Old Testament, Jewish, and Christian Conceptions*, edited by James M. Scott, 7–36. Leiden/New York: Brill, 1997.

Swarup, Paul. "Lamentations." In *South Asia Bible Commentary*, 1019–1030. India: Open Doors Publications, 2015.

Tiemeyer, Lena-Sofia. *For the Comfort of Zion the Geographical and Theological Location of Isaiah 40-55*. Leiden/Boston: Brill, 2011.

Thomas, Heath. "Lamentations in the Patristic Period." In *Great Is Thy Faithfulness?: Reading Lamentations as Sacred Scripture*, edited by Robin A. Parry and Heath Thomas, 113–119. Eugene, OR: Pickwick Publications, 2011.

Ubaldo, Lars Raymund Cortuna. "Dung-aw, pasyon at panagbiag: tatlong hibla ng pakasaritaan ti biag sa kasaysayang pangkalinangang Ilokano." A thesis submitted at the University of the Philippines, 2003.

Villanueva, Federico G. *The "Uncertainty of a Hearing": A Study of the Sudden Change of Mood in the Psalms of Lament*. Vol. 121 *VTSup*. Leiden: Brill, 2008.

Villaroman-Bautista, Violeta. "Spirituality and Resilience in Disaster Situations: Sources of Life and Strength in Critical Times." In *Walking with God: Christian Spirituality in the Asian Context*, edited by Charles R. Ringma and Karen Hollenbeck-Wuest, 164–183. Manila: Asian Theological Seminary and OMF Literature, 2014.

Westermann, Claus. *Lamentations: Issues and Interpretation*. Translated by Charles Muenchow. Edinburgh: T & T Clark, 1994.

Wilce, James MacLynn. *Crying Shame Metaculture, Modernity, and the Exaggerated Death of Lament*. Malden, MA/Oxford: Wiley-Blackwell, 2009.

Wilcox, Pete. "John Calvin's Interpretation of Lamentations." In *Great Is Thy Faithfulness?: Reading Lamentations as Sacred Scripture*, edited by Robin A Parry and Heath Thomas, 125–130. Eugene, OR: Pickwick Publications, 2011.

Wolterstorff, Nicholas. *Lament for a Son*. Grand Rapids, MI: Eerdmans, 1987.

Wright, Christopher J. H. *The Message of Lamentations: Honest to God*. Nottingham: IVP, 2015.

Zenger, Erich, and Linda M. Maloney. *A God of Vengeance? Understanding the Psalms of Divine Wrath*. Louisville, KY: Westminster John Knox Press, 1996.

Zimmerli, Walther. *Old Testament Theology in Outline*. Edinburgh: T & T Clark, 1978.

Asia Theological Association
54 Scout Madriñan St. Quezon City 1103, Philippines
Email: ataasia@gmail.com Telefax: (632) 410 0312

OUR MISSION

The Asia Theological Association (ATA) is a body of theological institutions, committed to evangelical faith and scholarship, networking together to serve the Church in equipping the people of God for the mission of the Lord Jesus Christ.

OUR COMMITMENT

The ATA is committed to serving its members in the development of evangelical, biblical theology by strengthening interaction, enhancing scholarship, promoting academic excellence, fostering spiritual and ministerial formation and mobilizing resources to fulfill God's global mission within diverse Asian cultures.

OUR TASK

Affirming our mission and commitment, ATA seeks to:

- **Strengthen** interaction through inter-institutional fellowship and programs, regional and continental activities, faculty and student exchange programs.
- **Enhance** scholarship through consultations, workshops, seminars, publications, and research fellowships.
- **Promote** academic excellence through accreditation standards, faculty and curriculum development.
- **Foster** spiritual and ministerial formation by providing mentor models, encouraging the development of ministerial skills and a Christian ethos.
- **Mobilize** resources through library development, information technology and infra-structural development.

To learn more about ATA, visit www.ataasia.com   or   Facebook /AsiaTheologicalAssociation

Langham Literature and its imprints are a ministry of Langham Partnership.

Langham Partnership is a global fellowship working in pursuit of the vision God entrusted to its founder John Stott –

to facilitate the growth of the church in maturity and Christ-likeness through raising the standards of biblical preaching and teaching.

Our vision is to see churches in the majority world equipped for mission and growing to maturity in Christ through the ministry of pastors and leaders who believe, teach and live by the Word of God.

Our mission is to strengthen the ministry of the Word of God through:
- nurturing national movements for biblical preaching
- fostering the creation and distribution of evangelical literature
- enhancing evangelical theological education

especially in countries where churches are under-resourced.

Our ministry

Langham Preaching partners with national leaders to nurture indigenous biblical preaching movements for pastors and lay preachers all around the world. With the support of a team of trainers from many countries, a multi-level programme of seminars provides practical training, and is followed by a programme for training local facilitators. Local preachers' groups and national and regional networks ensure continuity and ongoing development, seeking to build vigorous movements committed to Bible exposition.

Langham Literature provides majority world preachers, scholars and seminary libraries with evangelical books and electronic resources through publishing and distribution, grants and discounts. The programme also fosters the creation of indigenous evangelical books in many languages, through writer's grants, strengthening local evangelical publishing houses, and investment in major regional literature projects, such as one volume Bible commentaries like *The Africa Bible Commentary* and *The South Asia Bible Commentary*.

Langham Scholars provides financial support for evangelical doctoral students from the majority world so that, when they return home, they may train pastors and other Christian leaders with sound, biblical and theological teaching. This programme equips those who equip others. Langham Scholars also works in partnership with majority world seminaries in strengthening evangelical theological education. A growing number of Langham Scholars study in high quality doctoral programmes in the majority world itself. As well as teaching the next generation of pastors, graduated Langham Scholars exercise significant influence through their writing and leadership.

To learn more about Langham Partnership and the work we do visit **langham.org**